BRAIN,
MIND,
AND BEHAVIOR

BRAIN, MIND, AND BEHAVIOR

A New Perspective on Human Nature

DAVID L. ROBINSON

Foreword by H. J. Eysenck

PRAEGER

Westport, Connecticut
London

Library of Congress Cataloging-in-Publication Data

Robinson, David L.
    Brain, mind, and behavior : a new perspective on human nature /
    David L. Robinson ; foreword by H. J. Eysenck.
        p.   cm.
    Includes bibliographical references and index.
    ISBN 0–275–95468–4 (alk. paper)
    1. Personality.   2. Temperament.   3. Intellect.   4. Brain.
    5. Neuropsychology.   I. Title.
    BF698.R8544   1996
    155.2—dc20   95–43765

British Library Cataloguing in Publication Data is available.

Library of Congress Catalog Card Number: 95–43765
ISBN: 0–275–95468–4

First published in 1996

Praeger Publishers, 88 Post Road West, Westport, CT 06881
An imprint of Greenwood Publishing Group, Inc.

Printed in the United States of America

The paper used in this book complies with the
Permanent Paper Standard issued by the National
Information Standards Organization (Z39.48–1984).

10 9 8 7 6 5 4 3 2 1

Copyright Acknowledgments

The author and publisher gratefully acknowledge permission for use of the
following material:

Excerpts from Charles A. Spearman, *The Abilities of Man, Their Nature &
Measurement.* New York: AMS Press.

Every reasonable effort has been made to trace the owners of copyright materials
in this book, but in some instances this has proven impossible. The author and
publisher will be glad to receive information leading to more complete acknowledgments in subsequent printings of the book and in the meantime extend their
apologies for any omissions.

To
H. J. Eysenck, D. O. Hebb, and I. P. Pavlov

Who did much to help us understand the psychological significance of brain function

Canst thou not minister to a mind diseased,
Pluck from the memory a rooted sorrow,
Raze out the written troubles of the brain,
And with some sweet oblivious antidote
Cleanse the stuffed bosom of that perilous stuff
Which weighs upon the heart?

William Shakespeare
Macbeth V, iii

Contents

Illustrations

FIGURES

TABLES

Foreword

The theory of personality over the last fifty years or so has been tied down very much to either highly speculative psychoanalytic "dynamic" accounts or to endlessly repetitive psychometric studies of taxonomy involving correlational analysis and factor analysis. The demonstration in recent years that genetic factors are prominent in producing differences in personality has changed the climate greatly and has made much more acceptable than previously the notion that biological factors are important in the causation of such differences. This is true both on the side of cognitive personality differences (intelligence, special abilities) as on the side of noncognitive personality (temperament, character). The facts of genetic causation are now widely accepted and are supported by many large-scale investigations involving up to fifteen thousand pairs of twins, carried out in many different countries—from England to Scandinavia, from Australia to the United States.

Clearly, a link is required to connect the genes and chromosomes on the one side with the behavioral differences observed phenotypically on the other. Such mediating links must be found in human physiology, neuroanatomy, hormonal secretions, etc., and much work has been done in recent years to discover these missing links. Studies have used the EEG, averaged evoked potentials, contingent negative variation (CNV), positron emission tomography (PET), brain electrical activity mapping (BEAM) analysis and many other forms of measurement, which now present a formidable array of techniques, methods, and results for the student of personality. Much of this work is heuristic, lacking in sound theoretical formulation, and it is particularly gratifying to welcome in this book an author who has attempted to go back to first principles, and who has attempted to marry Pavlovian-type concepts with modern methods of measurement and analysis. To have done so in the study of both the cognitive and non-cognitive aspects of personality is particularly notable; few people have tried to use similar concepts in the analysis of both intellect and temperament.

Another important aspect of the book is its historical orientation. Modern workers typically have no knowledge of, or respect for earlier work, however seminal it may have been; recent handbooks of personality hardly mention the important theories put forward by Pavlov, or the equally important psychological experiments carried out in England by the London School under the guidance of Spearman. Robinson is well versed in this historical domain and succeeds in linking it with modern developments, in particular his highly technical experimental approach. His background in physics has enabled him to use these modern methods of refined electro-physiological measurement to the best advantage, and to use them to give empirical meaning and support to notions such as excitation and inhibition which formed an essential basis for Pavlovian theorizing.

Whatever their ultimate fate, Robinson's theories are certainly worthy of detailed consideration, and it is to be hoped that his results will be replicated and extended by others. If they stand up to such critical treatment, they certainly mark an important step forward in a field that is vital to the understanding of human behavior.

Professor H. J. Eysenck
Institute of Psychiatry
University of London

Preface

Brain, Mind, and Behavior describes new discoveries concerning the relationship between brain function and individual differences in human personality and intelligence. These findings and related theoretical developments provide new insights concerning the greatest mysteries of all—human nature and the human mind. The book should interest all who wish to know more about human nature, especially psychologists and those concerned with the psychological significance of neuroscience. It is essential reading for undergraduate and postgraduate psychology students with a main interest in personality and individual differences and for professional psychologists concerned with mental health, education, and human resource management where knowledge of personality and individual differences is of primary and fundamental importance. The more important claims that can be made for the book are enumerated below.

1. Empirical findings provide unequivocal support for the general direction or thrust of theories concerning the biological bases of personality and temperament that were developed earlier by Pavlov and Eysenck.

2. It has been possible to identify and resolve problems associated with the theories of Pavlov and Eysenck as well as to refine and greatly extend these to include the domain of intelligence.

3. For the first time, it has been possible to map out in a clear and unambiguous manner the neurological determinants of the major dimensions of personality and to show, after more than two millennia, the essential

validity of the ancient fourfold classification of temperaments into the melancholic, sanguine, phlegmatic, and choleric types.

4. The same fundamental dimensions of neurological variation determine the "structure" of intelligence, and with this new knowledge, it is possible to reconcile earlier conflicting notions of intelligence structure proposed by Spearman and Cattell.

5. There is support for a definition of intelligence in terms of the "availability of information," and it has been possible to specify in precise terms just how fundamental neurological differences mediating differences in cerebral "arousability" can influence different neurological processes that enable the acquisition, retention, and utilization of information. That is to say, the neurological processes that enable learning, memory, and attention are specified.

6. It has been possible to demonstrate how intelligence differences relate to personality or temperament differences and in this way to achieve the *first* integrated, detailed, and comprehensive explanation of brain, mind, and behavior relations.

7. In this book and in related articles in science journals, a new set of procedures and techniques is described which, for the first time, permits the *physically, neurologically, and psychologically meaningful* analysis of brain electrical responses generated by the activity of cerebral neurons. These data not only bear on questions of great psychological significance, but *they also yield the first systematic and empirically valid explanation of "alpha frequency" EEG activity and other related neurological phenomena.*

8. The new theory is related explicitly to the specialist areas of "experimental" psychology such as perception, memory, learning, motivation, and attention. It is suggested that the results of research in these areas have not been, and could not be, properly interpreted without reference to the individual differences detailed in this book.

9. Reference to the new theory demonstrates how Freud was led to erroneous conclusions, and alternative explanations are provided for the phenomena of chief interest to him.

10. Reference is made to the ideas of Jung and the "humanist" psychologists Maslow and Rogers. These theorists have addressed areas essentially untouched by Freud that relate in an important and interesting way to a new conception of "higher" cerebral emotions and the "archetypal" experiences that release these emotions: the emotions of love and hate that motivate all "self-transcending" behavior. There is here an explanation for the aesthetic appreciation and moral sense that allows people to discriminate beauty and

goodness from ugliness and evil and thereby to act in ways that are most characteristically human, if least well explained by existing psychological theories.

11. Twin studies have consistently indicated that genetic endowment strongly influences personality and intelligence, and there is recent evidence that this influence extends to include religious and political attitudes. The theory elaborated in this book explains precisely how genetic differences are translated through neurological systems into these psychological differences.

12. The whole of literature is made up of attempts to describe the most powerful archetypal scenarios and the responses to these scenarios of heroes and villains motivated by the self-transcending emotions of love and hate and not merely by the brutish and self-serving pursuit of pleasure or avoidance of pain that has been the bedrock of psychoanalysis and behaviorism. In recent times, many authors have recognized that the psychological conflict of humanity, our propensity for great creative achievements alongside the most pathologically destructive behaviors, has become a threat to the whole planet. In this book, the "human predicament" is explained by reference to the evolution of high intelligence and stronger self-transcending emotions. It is argued that these attributes initially enhanced our prospects for survival and led to the ascendancy of humankind over all other life-forms. Ultimately, however, these developments carry a sting in the tail, and they could be the seeds of our own destruction. As we create material and social environments that are artificial and alien, we not only suffer the more obvious physical consequences, such as asthma and cancer epidemics, but less obviously our genetically determined psychological responses to these alien material and social environments become increasingly inappropriate, destructive, and pathological.

13. Although not elaborated in great detail, the general theory formulated in this book provides the basis for a new, systematic, comprehensive, and neurologically based understanding of mental illness and the symptoms of mental illness. The methods of EEG analysis that are described here and in related articles in science journals provide the means for a simple test of the general health of the CNS. There is also the promise of precise neurological data and correspondingly unambiguous diagnoses and the possibility of systematic evaluation of the therapeutic effects of different drugs and procedures.

14. There are equally important pedagogic implications since it is possible to specify large and genetically determined differences in *modes* of learning and of the utilization of attention and recall which suggest that the

best educational environment for one temperament type may be the worst for another. Most important, it can also be inferred that the typical school environment is actually *the least suitable for the temperament type with lowest IQ and most in need of educational support and assistance.*

15. No less important than the medical and educational applications, there is a sure and certain basis for providing vocational guidance and for the determination of employee selection criteria which would guarantee major improvements in human resource management.

1

Introduction

Any account of the human brain or human behavior that omits reference to mind is clearly inadequate. However, if psychology without a psyche is nonsensical, it must also be acknowledged that the study of mind does involve some special difficulties precisely because subjective phenomena cannot be ignored. These difficulties are greatly exacerbated since those who study brain and behavior are inevitably influenced and constrained by concepts that have been adopted in the domain of the more elementary but better established physical sciences.

In particular, there is the canon that science should accumulate knowledge through the application of *objective* procedures to ensure that one investigator can always replicate the work of another and hopefully obtain similar results. Conceptually linked to this well-intentioned emphasis on the use of objective procedures is the unfortunate notion that knowledge has to do only with material objects as distinct from mental concepts, ideas, or beliefs; that it is only the objective that is real and has actual existence; and that true knowledge is something distinct from the sensations and emotions that people actually experience. These notions are evidently incorrect since there is no such thing as objective knowledge. An individual can only know or have any knowledge whatsoever by virtue of experiences that are entirely subjective.

As is well known, the distinction between objective and subjective relates back to the ideas of Locke and to his claim that there are real material things existing independently of the observer and that these have the primary *objective* qualities of size, shape, solidity, and motion. In contrast, it was suggested, objects do not really have color, taste, or scent. These are only secondary *subjective* qualities dependent on the observer. Here there is not even a mention of emotions. Presumably, emotions are regarded as entirely subjective and not in any way related to any properties or qualities of the external environment. The assumption, of course, is that all knowledge comes to us through the external milieu and through the agency of the senses.

Locke's claims and similar contemporary views must be rejected because knowing is synonymous with conscious experience and because conscious experience and knowledge have as much to do with evolution and genetic endowment as with contemporary environmental influence. Further, Locke's distinction between the primary and secondary qualities of objects is not valid since the perception of size, shape, solidity, and motion is no less secondary than the perception of color, taste, sound, and scent. All are mediated by the same or similar neurological processes and all derive from the secondary neurological representation of object properties.

Relying only on our own sensory impressions we are just as likely to disagree concerning the size of an object as we are to disagree concerning its color. The illusion that we can be more certain of the size of an object relates only to the ease with which we can refer to some standard or objective measure of extent. When Locke set down his ideas, spectrophotometers had not been invented. Now we can easily ascertain that under standard conditions a particular object will absorb certain frequencies of light while reflecting other frequencies and that it is perceived to have a corresponding color by all normal observers. Consequently, although the perception of color is entirely subjective, such perceptions constitute knowledge of real object properties and in this respect do not differ from perceptions of size, shape, and so on.

In the elementary physical sciences, where the focus of attention is on the material objects of the external milieu, one can sustain the illusion that knowledge may be distinguished from subjective experience. This is not possible in psychological science where the inner milieu of the mind or psyche cannot be ignored. If all knowledge is subjective, then it can hardly be suggested that the study of subjective experience is illegitimate. Once this is accepted, any legitimate difficulties concerning the study of mind can be recognized as arising solely from methodological considerations and from the requirement that one investigator should be able to replicate the observations of another.

It is an easy matter to establish that individuals with normal vision can detect light and distinguish different frequencies within the same range of frequencies. The same results will be obtained by different investigators, and on this basis we can state quite precisely what it is in the external environment that gives rise to "redness," "greenness," or "blueness" sensations. In effect, we can *objectively* establish the reality of these and all other sensations and emotions. Thus, although we cannot even begin to explain how human beings experience "redness," "pain," "love," "hatred," and so on, we cannot doubt the existence of such sensations and emotions.

Further, even if the ability to experience seems intimately bound up with the mystery of life itself, and may be something that we can never hope to understand, we can still observe that this ability depends on the integrity of particular neural processes and all available information indicates that the organization of mental experience is entirely determined by the operation of brain systems. Because brain systems determine the manner in which mental experience is organized, they also determine its meaning and thereby determine mind. That is to say, the *quality* of mental experience gives it the potential to have meaning and to motivate, but mind is not the great blooming buzzing confusion described by William James; it is the *organization* of mental experience imposed by brain systems and evident in terms of specific psychological processes such as perception, memory, attention, motivation, and learning. Ultimately, these specific processes are manifest in the integrated behavior of the whole individual as the more general psychological attributes, personality and intelligence. Thus, the title refers to neurological parameters that determine differences in the organized totality of psychological structures and processes that, in turn, determine differences in behavior.

While psychological structures and processes are manifestly and profoundly influenced by life experience, this can only be achieved through the operation of brain systems. Thus, it is no longer possible for psychologists to argue that the psyche of an individual can develop or be expressed in a way that is free from constraints imposed by the anatomy and physiology of the brain. Moreover, since the brain of one individual is not identical to that of another, there are good grounds for supposing that psychologically significant neurological parameters can be identified by seeking to ascertain whether and to what extent neurological variation is systematically related to psychological differences.

In my research, carried on over the last twenty years, I have adopted this general approach. It has proved extremely fruitful, and I have made some interesting and fundamental discoveries concerning the relationship between brain function and the human psyche. These empirical findings provide unequivocal support for the general direction or thrust of theories concerning the biological bases of personality and temperament that were developed earlier by Pavlov and Eysenck. Concurrently, it has been possible to identify and resolve problems associated with these theories as well as to refine and greatly extend them to include the domain of intelligence. For the first time, it has been feasible to map out in a clear and unambiguous manner the neurological determinants of the major dimensions of personality and to show, after more than two millennia, the validity of the ancient fourfold classification of temperaments. In addition, it can now be demonstrated how the same fundamental dimensions of neurological variation determine the structure of intelligence and how, with this new knowledge, it is possible to reconcile earlier notions of intelligence based mainly on the statistical analysis of test data. No less important, there is support for a definition of intelligence in terms of "the availability of information," and it has been possible to specify in precise terms just how the more fundamental neurological differences can influence different neurological processes mediating the acquisition, retention, and utilization of information. Finally, it has been possible to demonstrate how intelligence differences relate to personality or temperament differences and in this way to achieve the first integrated, detailed, and comprehensive explanation of brain, mind, and behavior relations.

To provide a proper historical context for the new discoveries and theoretical developments, Chapter 2 has been given over to consideration of Pavlov's study of brain-behavior relationships and to his ideas concerning the causation of temperament differences. In Chapter 3, Pavlov's conflicting findings concerning the "balance of excitation and inhibition" are reconciled and partly explained in terms of cerebral and brain-stem interaction. Some unresolved questions are identified and additional questions arise in Chapter 4 when the theory of brain-function that can best account for Pavlov's findings concerning temperament is compared with Eysenck's contemporary theory of the manner in which cerebral arousability determines personality differences.

In Chapter 5, a new method is described which permits the physically, neurologically, and psychologically meaningful analysis of brain electrical responses generated by the activity of cerebral neurons. New information about the manner in which functional properties of the brain relate to temperament, personality, and intelligence is discussed in Chapters 6, 7, and 8. These data resolve questions of fundamental theoretical significance and give rise to the new theory of brain, mind, and behavior relationships referred to above. In the first instance, this explains Pavlov's findings while refining and greatly extending Eysenck's theory of arousability.

Since the new theory also explains Spearman's g, or general intelligence factor, and provides new insights concerning the nature and structure of intelligence differences, and how intelligence relates to personality and temperament, there are especially strong reasons for reappraising Spearman's findings and ideas. These add to and greatly enrich this account of temperament, personality, and intelligence differences. Spearman's ability "factors" are discussed in Chapter 9, and his broader conception of intelligence and cognition is considered in Chapter 10.

Although most easily related to ideas that are associated with the systematic study and measurement of individual differences—as in the case of the concepts developed by Pavlov, Eysenck, and Spearman—the theory developed and elaborated in succeeding chapters also relates explicitly to phenomena studied in the specialist areas of "experimental" psychology such as perception, memory, learning, motivation, and attention. Indeed, it is difficult to imagine how the results of research in these areas could ever be properly interpreted without reference to the individual differences described herein.

The universality and general relevance of the new theory is further demonstrated in Chapter 11, where alternative explanations are derived for the psychological phenomena that most interested Freud. Many have criticized psychoanalytic theory, and much of this criticism may be valid, but no satisfactory alternative account has yet been offered to explain the observations on which Freud's theory is based. Such an account is provided in Chapter 11 where reference is also made to the ideas of Jung and of Maslow and Rogers. These latter theorists address areas essentially untouched by Freud that relate in an important and interesting way to a new conception of higher "cerebral" emotions. This conception of higher cerebral emotions offers an explanation for the aesthetic appreciation and moral sense that allows people to discriminate beauty and goodness from ugliness and evil and thereby to act in ways that are most characteristically human if least well explained by existing psychological theories.

The final chapter deals with the influence of genetic endowment on personality, temperament, and intelligence and illustrates how the new theory relates to and explains the results obtained in twin studies. More generally, this last chapter is concerned with what the new theory and related information tell us about the essential nature of human beings and with what Koestler has referred to as the human predicament. It is argued that the evolution of high intelligence, and of the cerebral emotions of love and hate, initially enhanced our prospects for survival and led to the ascendancy of humankind. Ultimately, however, this evolutionary development may contain the seeds of our own destruction because it has brought about radical and therefore toxic changes to the material and social environments.

We greatly underestimate our dependence on the environment, and despite the almost daily accumulation of new evidence, we fail to recognize that we are attuned to the "natural" environment and that *any* change or alteration is likely to have undesirable consequences. In the present account, it is suggested that human behavior is much more under genetically determined environmental control than we would like to imagine. It follows that as we create material and social environments that are artificial and alien, we not only suffer the more obvious physical consequences such as asthma and cancer epidemics but, less obviously, our genetically determined psychological responses to these alien material and social environments become increasingly inappropriate, destructive, and pathological.

2

Pavlov's Study of
Brain-Behavior Relationships

Pavlov's study of brain-behavior relationships led him to propose that in dogs it is possible to distinguish the four classical temperaments first described by Hippocrates and later by Galen. In simple contemporary terms, the sanguine and choleric temperaments are extraverted whereas the phlegmatic and melancholic temperaments are introverted. These types can be further differentiated since sanguine and phlegmatic individuals are emotionally stable whereas melancholic and choleric individuals are emotionally unstable. Pavlov suggested that these temperament differences are caused by differences in the functional properties of brain cells located in the cerebral cortex. Although he was never able to understand fully the nature of the proposed functional differences, or the exact manner in which they related to variation of temperament, the research carried on in his laboratories for some twenty-five years leaves little room to doubt the general proposition that temperament variation does indeed relate to differences in the functional characteristics of the central nervous system (Teplov, 1964).

The pioneering research on dogs carried on by Pavlov and his collaborators has an important and fundamental bearing on questions concerning the nature of differences in human temperament and personality (Claridge, 1967; Eysenck, 1957, 1967; Eysenck and Eysenck, 1985; Gray, 1964, 1979; Lynn, 1965; Mangan, 1980; Nebylitsyn, 1972; Pribram, 1968; Strelau, 1983; Robinson, 1982; Robinson, Gabriel, and Katchan, 1994; Zuckerman,

1994) and on related questions concerning the aetiology of mental illness (Claridge, 1995) and the nature of human intelligence (Robinson, 1989, 1991, 1993). Unfortunately, many of the theoretical and empirical problems encountered by Pavlov remain unresolved, and there is still no comprehensive theory that can explain all of the data that he accumulated.

What emerges from Pavlov's various publications is that attempts to demonstrate an exact correspondence between temperamental and neurological types were frustrated largely because of the enormous difficulty involved in the identification of behavioral indices that would unambiguously define neurological types. In contrast, temperamental types were easily recognized, and these were found to correspond closely to the ancient fourfold classification system of Hippocrates and Galen. This discovery is seldom given adequate emphasis, but even considered in isolation, it has great psychological significance. It is all the more significant since one is not dealing here with casual observation but with the systematic and careful study of individual animals carried on over very long periods of time.

THE FOUR TEMPERAMENTS

Pavlov's descriptions indicate that the four temperamental types can be readily distinguished in terms of a relatively small number of very obvious traits. The melancholic and phlegmatic types were characteristically inhibited in terms of their movements yet with no tendency to fall asleep when restrained and subjected to prolonged and monotonous experimental sessions. The melancholic type differed from the phlegmatic type in that animals in the former category were extremely fearful and anxious. In contrast, phlegmatic animals were remarkably unresponsive to their surroundings and did not enter into either friendly or antagonistic relations.

The choleric and sanguine types were easily distinguished from the melancholic and phlegmatic types because their behavior was typically uninhibited. The sanguine animals, like the melancholics, reacted quickly to the least stimulation but in a positive manner. They were extremely vivacious, always sniffing around and gazing at everything intently. Such animals became acquainted with people quickly and easily but often became annoying because they were so affectionate and demonstrative. According to Pavlov, they could never be made to keep quiet either by orders or by mild physical punishment. In stark contrast to their behavior when at liberty, the sanguine dogs had a marked tendency to fall asleep when restrained during experimental sessions and this despite frequent reinforcement.

Pavlov had much less to say about choleric animals, noting only that they were similar to the sanguine type but in most cases aggressive.

Pavlov's observations concerning the four temperaments can be summarized in terms of differences in the degree of behavioral inhibition, differences in susceptibility to sleep, and differences in the strength and character of emotional responses. Behavioral inhibition and susceptibility to sleep do not appear to be independent attributes, and there is already a clear indication that greater behavioral inhibition is associated with greater activation of brain systems that maintain the waking state. It is clear also that the strength and character of emotional responses must relate in some way to differences in behavioral inhibition since it is only inhibited animals that are fearful and anxious. Likewise, it is only uninhibited animals that are aggressive, or alternatively, affectionate and confident. In these terms, the melancholic and choleric animals appear to be at the opposite poles of a behavioral and emotional continuum which contrasts fearfulness and behavioral inhibition with aggressiveness and impulsivity. However, the fearful and inhibited character of the melancholic type may also be contrasted with the affectionate, confident, and uninhibited temperament of sanguine animals so that it is possible to suggest another behavioral and emotional continuum also involving the melancholic type.

The importance of the two contrasts just mentioned cannot be overemphasized, and ultimately it will be demonstrated that melancholics are actually extreme on two neurological dimensions with sanguine individuals at the opposite pole of one continuum and cholerics at the opposite pole of the other. *The key to understanding much that follows in succeeding chapters is to keep in mind this particular structure of temperament differences.*

The notion that there are just four temperamental types is perhaps not all that easy to accept, but this view has persisted for over two millennia and should not be dismissed lightly. What is implied by the fourfold classification scheme is simply that there are two main ways in which temperament can vary just as the two variables, height and weight, describe the most obvious differences in gross physical appearance. In both cases, the four combinations of extreme values of the two variables give rise to very distinctive and easily recognized types. Clearly, most individuals in a population would not be extreme in terms of typological attributes. Moreover, a finer grained analysis of individuals falling in any one of the four possible temperament categories would be expected to reveal differences on other psychological variables.

PAVLOV'S CLASSICAL CONDITIONING PROCEDURE

As is well known, the "classical conditioning" procedure developed by Pavlov involved the pairing of a "neutral" stimulus with an "unconditioned" stimulus which was normally either food powder or weak acid. When these unconditioned stimuli are placed in the mouth of an experimental subject, there is increased salivation. If a neutral stimulus, such as an auditory tone, is presented along with an unconditioned stimulus, on a number of occasions, the neutral stimulus also acquires the capacity to elicit a salivary response when subsequently presented without the unconditioned stimulus. The previously neutral stimulus has now become an excitatory "conditioned" stimulus.

If presentation of the excitatory conditioned stimulus is continued for a period without any reinforcement by the unconditioned stimulus, it eventually loses its excitatory effect and acquires the capacity to actively inhibit salivation. In fact, the excitatory conditioned stimulus becomes an inhibitory conditioned stimulus. An important point to note for future reference is that increased salivation is caused by *both* pleasant (food powder) and unpleasant (acid) stimuli. Thus, in the Pavlovian paradigm, an excitatory conditioned stimulus signals events that can be *either* pleasant or unpleasant. It is also noted that when Pavlov refers to cortical processes of excitation and inhibition, to account for the dynamics of salivary responding, *cortical* excitation is inferred to explain *behavioral* excitation while *cortical* inhibition is inferred to explain *behavioral* inhibition. However, as Pavlov himself acknowledged, the actual character of the neural systems was unknown. Consequently one cannot assume an identity between the excitatory and inhibitory processes inferred by Pavlov and *neural* excitation and inhibition processes as these are understood today.

THE TEMPERAMENTS AND CLASSICAL CONDITIONING

In a way that parallels the differences in *general* behavioral excitation and inhibition described earlier, the first of Pavlov's three successive theoretical formulations was based on data which indicated that in sanguine dogs it was easier to excite a salivary response with a conditioned stimulus than it was to inhibit such a response. In contrast, with melancholic animals, it was relatively difficult to elicit a salivary response with a conditioned stimulus but once reinforcement was discontinued the stimulus quickly acquired the capacity to inhibit responses. Thus, the sanguine type was described as a specialist in excitation whereas the melancholic type was a specialist in inhibition.

In the second of the three systems of classification, and the last one based primarily on the relative balance or imbalance of excitatory and inhibitory processes, the choleric type was substituted for the sanguine type as the specialist in excitation (Teplov, 1964, pp. 17–18). The reasons for this change are not made explicit but are clearly related to results obtained using techniques designed to produce a "collision" between excitation and inhibition. For example, when the frequency difference between conditioned excitatory and inhibitory tone stimuli was progressively reduced, so that discrimination became very difficult, there were profound pathological disturbances in the behavior of choleric and melancholic animals that could persist for weeks and even months. More specifically, there was a general breakdown in the capacity of these animals to respond differentially to excitatory and inhibitory conditioned stimuli. For choleric animals, all stimuli had an excitatory effect, whereas, for melancholic animals all stimuli had an inhibitory effect. These pathological disturbances were not confined to responses elicited by specific conditioned stimuli. Choleric animals became generally very excitable and irritable, whereas melancholic animals became more than usually inhibited and unresponsive.

These results suggested to Pavlov that in choleric animals the excitatory process was more effective and in melancholic animals the inhibitory process was more effective. The question arises: Why was this not also apparent in normal circumstances when the data collected over an extended period indicated that sanguine animals rather than choleric animals were the masters of excitation? Furthermore, since the method normally employed to form excitatory and inhibitory conditioned responses also actually involves competition between excitatory and inhibitory processes, there is every reason to expect comparable results.

It is suggested here that the reason for the apparent inconsistency is probably related to the fact that, in Pavlov's conception of excitation and inhibition, no distinction was made between the effects of conditioned stimuli that signaled pleasant and unpleasant events. As noted earlier, an excitatory conditioned stimulus was one that could elicit a salivary response irrespective of the nature of the unconditioned stimulus, which could be either food powder or acid. Likewise, an inhibitory stimulus was one that could inhibit responses to signals of either negative or positive events. Now it happens that one of the characteristics most often associated with the sanguine temperament is optimism. This suggests greater sensitivity to signals of positive or pleasant events and less sensitivity to signals of negative or unpleasant events. Indeed, Pavlov's own descriptions of sanguine animals indicate that this is so. The opposite is true in the case of the melancholic temperament, where characteristic and unrealistic pessimism suggests greater sensitivity to signals of negative events and less sensitivity to signals of positive events. Again, Pavlov's own descriptions of the behavior of melancholic animals indicates that this is the case. Failing initially to distinguish excitatory conditioned stimuli signaling food powder from those signaling acid, and regarding these as essentially equivalent, Pavlov and his associates actually used meat powder as an unconditioned stimulus much more often than acid. It can therefore be argued that the true or actual basis for Pavlov's first formulation was that sanguine animals responded much more readily to signals of pleasant events, and these responses were subsequently difficult to inhibit, whereas melancholic animals responded much less readily to signals of pleasant events and these responses were easily inhibited.

From the foregoing, it can be suggested that *Pavlov's first and second theoretical formulations involved two quite distinct contrasts involving different dimensions of neurological variation.* In the first case, sanguine dogs are contrasted with melancholics on the basis of differential sensitivity to signals of positive and negative events, and not as Pavlov thought in terms of differences in the *general* effectiveness of excitatory and inhibitory conditioned stimuli and irrespective of the character of the unconditioned stimuli. In the second classification system, based on results obtained using collision techniques, choleric animals are contrasted with melancholic animals. Here there is no reason to reject Pavlov's claim that this does reflect a general predominance of excitation or inhibition, respectively, insofar as these terms relate to behavioral excitation or inhibition.

Pavlov's dilemma was that he had formulated the single principle of excitation-inhibition balance, but the data sets obtained using different procedures could not both be accommodated by this single principle. At this point he had the option of rejecting his theory or rejecting one of his data sets. He chose the latter course, keeping the original principle but effectively relating it only to the data obtained using the collision techniques. Clearly, this is not a satisfactory solution, and ultimately any theory accounting for Pavlov's findings must explain both the original data and also the data obtained using the collision techniques.

THE TEMPERAMENTS AND "STRENGTH" OF THE NERVOUS SYSTEM

As Pavlov and his associates progressively developed new techniques and accumulated related data, the emphasis gradually shifted from those that indicated the relative influence of excitatory and inhibitory conditioned stimuli to those that indicated differences in the "strength" or "working capacity" of nervous processes. The meaning of Pavlov's strength concept is perhaps best indicated by the related measurement techniques. One of the most favored indexes of strength was based on changes in the magnitude of the salivary response that resulted from changes in stimulus intensity. What Pavlov and his colleagues discovered was that there is a fairly simple and direct relationship between the intensity of a stimulus "input" and the magnitude of a corresponding response "output." As stimulus intensity increases, there is a corresponding increase in response magnitude up to some upper limit. Beyond this upper limit, further increases of stimulus intensity cause a reduction in response magnitude. This reduction in response magnitude was attributed to a "protective" inhibitory process. Subjects were regarded as having a "weak" nervous system when response magnitudes increased more rapidly with increasing stimulus intensities and the upper limit of response magnitude occurred at lower stimulus intensities. When response magnitudes increased less rapidly, and the upper limit occurred at higher stimulus intensities, subjects were said to have strong nervous systems. With this procedure, melancholic animals were found to have weak or more reactive nervous systems whereas sanguine animals had strong or less reactive nervous systems.

An undoubted advantage of the procedure just described is that the effect can be linked more clearly and directly with intrinsic nervous system properties since it does not appear to relate in any way to prior learning experience. Equally important, Pavlov's use of the salivary response excludes effects associated with the voluntary control of behavior that would preclude any explanation of response differences in terms only of nervous system properties. Today, the procedure used by Pavlov may seem crude as compared with the recordings that can be made from single cells using microelectrodes but, in fact, Pavlov's approach provides information about the way in which the brain functions as a whole integrated unit whereas the latter only provides information about individual neurons. Ultimately, differences in strength formed the main basis for Pavlov's third and final typological classification, details of which were first published shortly before his death in 1936 (Pavlov, 1955, p. 313). In this final classification system, the melancholic and sanguine types are contrasted purely on the basis of strength, but what is confusing vis-à-vis his earlier formulations is that the melancholic and sanguine animals are both now regarded as having balanced processes of excitation and inhibition. In effect, there is now a complete reversal of the first formulation when the sanguine and melancholic types were regarded as unbalanced types and the "masters" of excitation and inhibition respectively. Again the reasons for this second change are not adequately considered in any of Pavlov's publications.

What could possibly have induced Pavlov, in his final formulation, to ignore or set aside all of the data accumulated from about 1910 to at least 1927?—data which indicated predominance of inhibition over excitation in melancholic animals. Even more puzzling, what now led to his quite definite assertion that sanguine and melancholic animals had equilibrated processes of excitation and inhibition?

Pavlov did have some grounds for doubting his earlier *conclusions,* but these certainly did not justify the outright rejection of all his earlier *findings.* More revealing is the firm conviction now that melancholic and sanguine types have *balanced* processes of excitation and inhibition. Although Pavlov does not explain the empirical grounds for his conclusions concerning balance in the final theoretical formulation, it is clear that these derived from data obtained using measures of strength. This third approach to the evaluation of excitation-inhibition balance again produced results that were inconsistent with earlier findings. As before, Pavlov retained the simple principle of excitation-inhibition balance and dealt with the inconsistency by setting aside or ignoring his earlier findings. Again it must be stated that this is not a satisfactory solution. The single principle of excitation-inhibition balance was clearly inadequate, and a theory is required that can account for all of the empirical findings.

In particular, *the required theory must specify one neurological continuum that contrasts melancholic and sanguine individuals. Another continuum must be specified that contrasts melancholics and cholerics.* The outline of such a theory will be worked out in the next two chapters.

3

Theoretical Integration of Pavlov's Findings

The present analysis suggests that the sanguine type can first be contrasted with the melancholic type in that the former is more sensitive to signals of pleasant events and less sensitive to signals of unpleasant events, while the opposite state of affairs applies to melancholics. There is also a contrast between these two types in that sanguine animals have less reactive or stronger nervous processes with equal strength or reactivity in the case of excitatory and inhibitory conditioned stimuli. Melancholic animals have more reactive or weaker nervous processes but again with an equal degree of weakness or reactivity with respect to excitatory and inhibitory conditioned stimuli. Finally, there is a contrast between choleric and melancholic animals which relates to results obtained using the collision techniques. According to Pavlov, these results indicate predominance of excitation over inhibition in choleric animals with predominance of inhibition over excitation in melancholics. Here it must be assumed that excitation-inhibition balance refers to something quite distinct from excitation-inhibition balance assessed using the strength procedures.

THE STRENGTH AND COLLISION TECHNIQUES: CEREBRAL REACTIVITY VERSUS BRAIN-STEM INHIBITION

In fact, a distinction can be made between the strength or reactivity of specific neural pathways, activated by conditioned stimuli, that project via the cerebrum to excite or inhibit salivary responses, and the influence of neural systems that can have a general excitatory or inhibitory effect on *all* responses. The existence of such systems was strongly indicated by the pathological general effects on responding of the collision techniques used by Pavlov. Moreover, the discovery that excitatory and inhibitory stimuli could generate aftereffects which altered general levels of responding also points to the involvement of systems capable of regulating general levels of neural activation or arousal.

An important difference between the strength index and earlier procedures is that the former is a measure of *relative* differences in response magnitude whereas the latter relate to *absolute* differences. Differences in absolute magnitude would reflect the combined influence of all neural systems involved in the processing of an input to produce an output. This is not the case when differences in response magnitude are assessed as a function of changes in stimulus intensity, since this relative measure excludes any effects that are common to responses obtained with high and low intensity stimuli. Thus, it is to be expected that procedures based on relative and absolute measurement of response amplitude will emphasize effects related to different stages in processing.

It will be recalled that, in melancholics, the strength measure indicates that neural processes mediating the input-output relationship are *more reactive* whereas the earlier procedures indicate that in melancholic animals *it is relatively difficult to excite responses.* This apparent contradiction can be explained if it is accepted that the relative strength measure differs in a way that reflects the reactivity of cerebral pathways activated by conditioned stimuli but excludes the global inhibitory influence of the cerebrum on brain stem processes, including the salivary nuclei, that would have an equal or common effect on responses to stimuli of different intensities.

In contrast, the absolute response magnitudes associated with the collision technique would reflect the degree of brain-stem inhibition. Since greater reactivity of the cerebrum would result in greater inhibition of the brain stem, there is every reason to anticipate apparently opposite and contradictory results using the strength and collision techniques. This explanation is consistent with the contemporary knowledge of neurological arousal systems that has accumulated over the last four decades. In an authoritative review of research on processes that regulate global levels of brain arousal or activation, Magoun (1963) concluded that:

Many contributions point to the existence of a non-specific thalamocortical system, the low-frequency excitation of which evokes large slow waves as well as recruiting responses and spindle bursts in the EEG . . . this system appears to manage all the Pavlovian categories of internal inhibition of higher nervous activity . . . it is now possible to identify a thalamocortical mechanism for internal inhibition, capable of modifying activity of the brain partially or globally. (173–174)

The reports of the earliest studies emphasized the role of an undifferentiated, ascending, reticular activating system mediating global changes in levels of cerebral activation or arousal. In contrast, the later findings referred to by Magoun revealed that the reticular substance extending into the thalamus forms part of a diffuse thalamocortical system that has a global inhibitory effect on the brain-stem reticular formation. Here it is important to note that the salivary nuclei, producing the responses most studied by Pavlov, are actually located in the brain stem and are therefore subject to the global inhibitory influence of the cerebrum.

This contemporary knowledge of brain arousal systems helps to reconcile the results obtained by Pavlov and his associates using different procedures, but it is also possible to suggest how very strong stimulation can cause "protective" inhibition. That is to say, if very strong stimulation can cause a more widespread or general activation of the cerebrum than is usually the case, and from Magoun's account this appears to be so, then the correspondingly greater inhibition of brain-stem processes can account for a reduction in response amplitudes at high stimulus intensities.

PAVLOV'S CONCEPTION OF THALAMOCORTICAL AND BRAIN-STEM INTERACTION

It is probable that with a little more time, Pavlov would have recognized the significance of thalamocortical and brain-stem interaction vis-à-vis the data obtained using his different procedures. He had correctly identified the cerebrum as the organ mediating conditioned connections or associations between stimuli. In his words, "a grandiose mosaic, upon which are distributed, at a given moment, a huge number of external (and internal) excitations, either stimulating or inhibiting the various activities of the organism" (Pavlov, 1930, p. 212).

In unparalleled fashion, he and his collaborators systematically mapped out the dynamics of cerebral function showing how the formation and interaction of temporary conditioned connections permits constant and fine-grained adjustments and adaptation to ever-changing and fluctuating environmental circumstances. Having no doubt whatsoever that conditioned connections were formed in the cerebrum—and this has been confirmed by subsequent research—he naturally assumed that the corresponding excitatory and inhibitory processes were located there also. In later publications this view had begun to change. There was an explicit recognition that thalamocortical and brain-stem interaction could influence conditioned responses in a way that points towards the explanation proposed here to reconcile data obtained using the collision and strength techniques.

According to Pavlov (1930),

[the] cerebral hemispheres, in some manner, overcome the described inertia of the subcortical centers with respect both to excitation and inhibition, since in a large number of cases the hemispheres must stimulate the organism to activity or to stop one or another of its activities through the intermediary of subcortical centers. . . . the simplest case is when the hemispheres gradually accumulate inhibitions, which become strong enough to overcome the direct strong excitation of subcortical centers. Indeed, we saw in our experiments more than once that long applied and intensive inhibition in the hemispheres may strongly hold back the effect of the unconditioned stimulus. Thus, food which is already in the mouth may not provoke salivation for a long while; thus, also, was it frequently observed that *chronic excitation of the cortex, following an operation, totally inhibits the activity of the subcortical centers for a considerable period of time*: the animals become entirely blind and deaf, whereas animals totally deprived of the hemispheres react, although in a limited way, to a strong luminous stimulus and especially distinctly to a sound stimulus. One may also easily imagine that *the cerebral hemispheres excited to a certain tonus throughout its whole mass, under the influence of a number of excitations reaching them, exert an inhibitory action upon the subcortical centers* . . . and thus lighten the load for themselves [of] every special additional inhibition of these centers. (214–215, emphasis added)

Clearly, Pavlov was, latterly at least, aware of the global inhibitory influence of the cerebrum or thalamocortical system on subcortical centers and it is even explicit that chronically high levels of thalamocortical excitation cause greater subcortical inhibition with profound behavioral consequences. Pavlov did not specify particular subcortical processes, but since most of his work involved measurement of the salivary responses, and since the salivary nuclei are located in the brain stem, it is clear that when he refers to inhibition of subcortical centers he is often if not always referring to inhibition of brain-stem processes.

In a way that foreshadows discovery of the brain-stem reticular activating system some thirty years later, he goes on to discuss the reciprocal influence of subcortical centers on the cerebral hemispheres. After reviewing the effects on conditioned responses of a number of procedures, described as the first tentative experimental approach to questions concerning the interaction of cortical and subcortical centers, Pavlov (1930, p. 215) suggests that "the active state of the hemispheres is being continually maintained by excitations coming from subcortical centers."

SOME UNRESOLVED QUESTIONS

Returning again to the specific data sets on which Pavlov based his successive temperament theories, it can be suggested that melancholic animals are characterized by greatest thalamocortical reactivity or sensitivity and also greatest inhibition of brain-stem processes. However, Pavlov's findings also imply that the degree of brain-stem inhibition is not wholly determined by thalamocortical reactivity. This is so because sanguine animals have the least reactive thalamocortical processes, but the results obtained using the collision techniques suggest that it is choleric, not sanguine, animals that have least inhibition of brain-stem processes. To account for this, there must be some factor or factors, additional to thalamo-cortical reactivity, that influence the degree of brain-stem inhibition.

Finally, it is noted that in this attempt to account for all of Pavlov's major findings relating to temperament differences, there is as yet no neurological process to explain differential responding to signals of pleasant and unpleasant events that is thought to be the true basis for Pavlov's first formulation and the original contrast between sanguine and melancholic types. This process must relate in some way to the differences in strength that Pavlov finally used to distinguish these two types, but no suggestions concerning the mechanism involved can be derived from Pavlov's research or from contemporary knowledge of the global interaction of the cerebrum and brain-stem systems.

In the next chapter the temperament differences described by Pavlov are related to contemporary knowledge of human personality variation. Here the work of H. J. Eysenck is of crucial importance because quantifiable dimensions of human personality variation have been established and these can be linked directly and unequivocally to the four temperament types of antiquity. Eysenck's theory of personality is particularly useful and interesting because, like Pavlov, he explains personality or temperament differences in neurological terms.

4

The Temperaments and Eysenck's Theory of Personality

THE TEMPERAMENTS AND CONTEMPORARY PERSONALITY DIMENSIONS

In human subjects, the systematic description and measurement of personality differences has progressed to the point where there is no longer any room to doubt the existence of personality dimensions that relate meaningfully to the ancient fourfold classification scheme adopted by Pavlov to describe temperament differences in his experimental animals. Research carried on over the past five decades and across different cultures indicates the universal validity of a small number of personality dimensions that can be reliably measured when properly constructed self-report questionnaires are administered under standard conditions (Eysenck and Eysenck, 1985). This is especially so in the case of the introversion-extraversion and neuroticism (emotional instability versus emotional stability) dimensions, where the four combinations of extreme scores correspond exactly to the four temperament types of antiquity (Eysenck and Eysenck, 1985, p. 50).

As indicated earlier, the choleric and melancholic types are extraverted and introverted, respectively, but in both cases neuroticism scores are high, indicating emotional instability and a predisposition to neurotic breakdown. The sanguine and phlegmatic types are also extraverted and introverted, respectively, but here neuroticism scores are low, indicating emotional stability.

EYSENCK'S THEORY OF THALAMOCORTICAL AROUSABILITY

The link between Pavlov's research on the neurological bases of temperament differences and contemporary research on personality variation is not confined to the descriptive level since H. J. Eysenck has for many years propounded the theory that introverts have typically higher levels of thalamocortical arousal or activation than extraverts. With other researchers working within the same general theoretical framework, he has amassed a very large body of indirect evidence which suggests that this is indeed the case (Eysenck, 1957, 1967; Eysenck and Eysenck, 1975; Eysenck and Eysenck, 1985). Although Eysenck's early thinking on this question demonstrates that he was influenced by Pavlov's ideas, it is especially noteworthy that whereas Pavlovian cortical excitatory and inhibitory processes actually correspond to behavioral excitation and inhibition, this is not so in the case of Eysenck's formulation.

In Eysenck's theory, introverted individuals (that is, the melancholic and phlegmatic types) have high levels of cortical excitation or arousal, *which causes behavioral inhibition*. In contrast, the extraverted individuals (that is, the choleric and sanguine types) have low levels of cortical excitation or arousal, *which causes behavioral excitability or lack of inhibition*. Thus, Eysenck's explanation for introversion-extraversion differences is consistent with contemporary knowledge of the relationship between thalamocortical and brain-stem processes—the same knowledge used earlier to reconcile results obtained with Pavlov's strength and collision techniques. It follows that there is some overlap between Eysenck's theory of introversion-extraversion and the theory so far elaborated to account for Pavlov's findings. Indeed, it must be acknowledged that the development of the latter owes much to prior familiarity with Eysenck's ideas and concepts just as the inspiration for much that follows can be attributed to his penetrating insights.

PAVLOV, EYSENCK, INTROVERSION-EXTRAVERSION, AND NEUROTICISM

Eysenck proposes that *all* introverts have higher levels of cortical arousability and therefore greater inhibition of brain-stem processes. The converse is suggested for *all* extraverts. In contrast, the results on which Pavlov's second and third formulations are based suggest that it is only melancholics or neurotic introverts that are characterized by very high thalamocortical arousability and correspondingly strong inhibition of brain-stem processes. As already noted, the results obtained using Pavlov's collision technique suggest that it is only choleric individuals, or neurotic extraverts that have very low levels of brain-stem inhibition and this implies lowest thalamocortical arousability. There is, of course, the anomaly that Pavlov's strength data indicate lowest thalamocortical arousability in the case of stable extraverts, which is to say, the sanguine rather than choleric type. This is counterintuitive since one would expect emotional instability and neuroticism at the extremes of the normal range of thalamocortical arousability. Melancholic and choleric individuals are emotionally unstable, but sanguine individuals are not. Foreshadowing results that are yet to be discussed, it is noted that the strength measure only relates to one aspect of thalamocortical arousability, and sanguine individuals are not actually extreme in terms of *overall* thalamocortical arousability. Thus, there is some reason to question the proposition that the fundamental difference between all extraverts and all introverts is determined by thalamocortical arousability.

While the explanation proposed to account for Pavlov's findings cannot accommodate the proposition that variation of thalamocortical arousability is the only or fundamental factor responsible for introversion-extraversion differences, it does suggest that differences in arousability determine differences in neuroticism or emotional stability. That is to say, neuroticism or emotional instability can be attributed to either very high arousability, in the case of melancholics, or very low arousability, in the case of cholerics.

This contrasts with Eysenck's explanation of neuroticism in terms of activation of the limbic system and of the sympathetic division of the autonomic nervous system. It might be suggested that very high levels of thalamocortical activation could result in greater sympathetic activation. If this were indeed the case, then Eysenck's explanation would correspond closely to the explanation based on Pavlov's data for neuroticism or emotional instability in the case of melancholics. Very low thalamocortical arousability, in the case of neurotic extraverts or choleric individuals, is less easily associated with high levels of sympathetic activation, although it is not inconceivable that this might indeed occur when there is extreme disinhibition of brain-stem processes.

Clearly, Pavlov's findings cannot be completely reconciled with Eysenck's conception of the neurological bases of introversion-extraversion and neuroticism. The importance of thalamocortical arousability is suggested in both cases, but there is disagreement as to the exact role and causal status of this variable with respect to temperament and personality differences. Also, as already noted, a theory accounting for the data supporting Pavlov's second and third formulations must refer to at least two dimensions or aspects of thalamocortical arousability and not just one. Finally, the data supporting Pavlov's first formulation must be explained if we are to understand one of the most obvious and fundamental differences in the behavior of the melancholic and sanguine type, namely, differential responsiveness to signals of pleasant and unpleasant events.

It is appropriate now to consider further the role of the diffuse thalamocortical system in the determination of fundamental psychological differences. This is taken up in the next chapter where a new method is described that allows the fundamental functional characteristics of this system to be determined directly from analysis of EEG responses. In subsequent chapters data will be described which show just how these functional differences determine differences in personality, temperament, and intelligence.

5

Thalamocortical Activity and the EEG

MOLAR EEG EFFECTS OF NEURAL EXCITATION AND INHIBITION

As already discussed, Pavlov's three formulations accounting for temperament differences were based on the view that the causal processes of excitation and inhibition were located in the cerebral cortex. This conviction derived from the knowledge, subsequently confirmed, that conditioned responses cannot be retained or acquired by decerebrate animals.

Latterly, it is clear, he came to recognize the profound psychological significance of differences in the relative influence of thalamocortical and subcortical processes, and, it must be assumed, given a little more time, this knowledge would have enabled him to reconcile the data obtained using the collision and strength techniques. That is to say, he would have come to recognize that the strength techniques indicated differences in thalamocortical reactivity whereas the collision techniques indicated differences in the degree of brain-stem inhibition. As noted earlier, the relationship between these variables should reflect the fact that *greater reactivity or excitability of the thalamocortical system determines greater brain-stem inhibition and greater inhibition of conditioned salivary responses.*

The most relevant recent research concerning the global interaction of thalamocortical and brain-stem arousal systems was reviewed by Magoun (1963). As already mentioned, these studies led Magoun to identify the diffuse thalamocortical system with the neurological processes inferred by

Pavlov while at the same time demonstrating that the activity of this system is manifest in the EEG. The clear implication here is that from the analysis of EEG activity it should, in principle, be possible to obtain information concerning differences in the functional properties of the diffuse thalamo-cortical system, and that such differences should relate systematically to personality or temperament differences.

Simple as this proposition might seem, there is the considerable problem that conventional EEG procedures confound the activity of different neural systems as well as confounding the activity of excitatory and inhibitory neurons. There is also no basis for making a distinction between differences in thalamocortical activity or arousal that relate to intrinsic functional properties of the cerebrum and differences determined by other agencies, especially the brain stem arousal system, that from moment to moment can alter the state of activation of the cerebrum.

To overcome these problems, I developed and applied a new technique for the analysis of EEG responses (Robinson, 1982, 1983, 1989, 1993). With this procedure, it is possible to obtain more reliable measures of EEG differences and to evaluate a variety of physical effects that can be related to the known functional characteristics of excitatory and inhibitory neurons of the diffuse thalamocortical system. These physical effects are analogous to the "capacitance" and "inductance" of electronics and may be understood in terms of differences in the relative effectiveness of neural excitation and neural inhibition at low and high frequencies of stimulation.

It is now generally accepted that EEG activity reflects aggregate extracel-lular potential changes associated with excitatory postsynaptic potentials (EPSPs) and inhibitory postsynaptic potentials (IPSPs). These postsynaptic potentials are caused by the arrival of individual neural impulses at the synaptic junctions which link the axon of one neuron with the soma or dendritic processes of another. As is well known, the arrival of an impulse at a synaptic junction causes the release of a neurotransmitter substance into the synaptic cleft, which then opens gates or channels in the adjacent cell membrane. This allows positively or negatively charged ions to flow into or out of the cell, which "receives" the neural impulse in a way that is determined by preexisting electrical and ion concentration gradients. Some axons release an excitatory transmitter substance, and the effect is to cause a small increase or depolarization of the intracellular potential, which is transient but persists for a period of milliseconds. If enough EPSPs occur in a given period, the summation of these small potential changes can increase the intracellular potential to the point where an action potential is generated, and the "stimulated" cell thereby transmits an impulse to other neurons. In contrast, some axons release an inhibitory transmitter substance, and here the net effect of transmembrane ionic currents is to reduce the intracellular potential of the neuron receiving the neural impulse. In this case the effect is to inhibit the generation of action potentials.

The procedure that I developed and applied was specifically designed to distinguish these opposed effects of neural excitation and neural inhibition. This can be achieved by the analysis of EEG responses to systematic manipulation of the frequency of peripheral stimulation, just as analogous capacitance and inductance effects can be identified and quantified in electrical circuits using similar procedures. Notably, such capacitance and inductance effects can be identified and quantified *even when nothing is known of the precise construction details of the corresponding capacitors and inductors*.

THE MOLECULAR BASIS OF MOLAR EEG EFFECTS

EPSPs and IPSPs are generated in the same or similar neurons and are therefore both influenced by the same or similar conditions. Thus, it is mainly the differential effects of excitatory and inhibitory neurotransmitters that ensure opposite effects in the case of excitation and inhibition.

Within the normal operational range of neurons, EPSPs are necessarily smaller and less effective at high frequencies of stimulation, since the electrical gradient that causes EPSPs is *reduced* when neurons are firing at a higher rate. In contrast, IPSPs are more effective when a neuron is generating action potentials at a higher rate. In this case, the greater than usual depolarization of the neuron *increases* the electrical gradient that causes IPSPs so that these are correspondingly larger and more effective (Eccles, 1969). What these known properties of neurons indicate is that when reciprocally connected cells form the closed loops or circuits, that alone can account for sustained autonomous activity of cerebral neurons, there will be a particular frequency of stimulation where the frequency-dependent "impedances" associated with inhibition and excitation cancel out and response magnitude is therefore greatest. At higher frequencies of stimulation, the impedance associated with excitation exceeds that associated with inhibition, and there will be a reduction in response magnitude. At low frequencies of stimulation, impedance associated with inhibition is greater than that associated with excitation, and here also response amplitude will be reduced.

In this way, it is possible to explain how molecular processes, when synchronized by peripheral stimulation, can be related to molar EEG frequency response curves (Robinson, 1983). Averaging across individuals, EEG response amplitude is greatest at a peripheral stimulation frequency of 10.10 Hz. It is noted that this "natural" frequency average corresponds closely to the average "alpha" frequency of 10.08 Hz that is apparent in spontaneous EEG recordings, and the respective standard deviations are also very similar. The oscillatory character of the spontaneous EEG, and the tendency to oscillate at a particular alpha frequency, can both be accounted for in terms of closed neural circuits and the relative influence of neural excitation and inhibition (Robinson, 1983).

ANALYSIS OF THALAMOCORTICAL ACTIVITY

People differ in terms of alpha frequency and in terms of the related frequency of peripheral visual stimulation that results in maximum EEG response amplitude. The shape of the "frequency-response" curves obtained for different individuals can be explained in terms of the relative effectiveness of excitation and inhibition, with more effective inhibition determining the occurrence of maximum response amplitude at frequencies below about 10.25 Hz and more effective excitation determining maximum response amplitude at frequencies above about 10.25 Hz. Close to this particular frequency, there is a balance of excitation and inhibition. A theoretical curve can be fitted to the EEG response amplitudes obtained for a given individual at different frequencies of peripheral stimulation (Robinson, 1983). By fitting such curves, it is possible to obtain *separate* estimates for the effectiveness, reactivity, or responsiveness of excitatory and inhibitory processes.

A third constant, analogous to resistance in an electrical circuit, can be ascertained, and this quantifies any general influence on thalamocortical responsiveness that is not frequency dependent and not associated with specific thalamocortical processes of excitation and inhibition. Because this is so, and in the light of other considerations that will not be detailed here, the third constant has been associated with agencies external to the thalamocortical system. Although external, these agencies can nevertheless alter the "gain" or arousability of the thalamocortical system in response to changing environmental circumstances or to the requirements of basic biological processes such as regulation of the sleep-wakefulness cycle. In particular, the third constant is thought to reflect the influence of the brain-stem reticular activating system, which is known to have a general influence on thalamocortical arousability.

As might be expected, the third "constant" can be less reliably determined than the excitation and inhibition constants. This is attributed to the fact that the influence of the brain-stem arousal system on thalamocortical activation varies considerably as a function of external and internal circumstances. Despite this variability, the third constant does have considerable psychological significance, but, equally important, it allows a clear distinction to be made between transient changes in levels of cortical activation and static differences in responsiveness that relate to the fixed intrinsic properties of thalamocortical neurons. As a result, the latter can be determined with far greater precision than would otherwise be possible.

The three constants that quantify fundamental functional differences in the operation of the diffuse thalamocortical system can be used to calculate two parameters that in the domain of systems theory provide a comprehensive summary description of the dynamic character of systems analogous to the one of interest here. When reference is made to dynamic character, one is thinking about the way a system behaves and, in effect, about the "arousability" of a system. Thus, in terms of what is known about the physical characteristics of systems in general, it is clear that any systematic and comprehensive description of thalamocortical arousability must refer to two arousability parameters or dimensions and not just one.

In the closed neural loops or circuits that constitute the diffuse thalamocortical system, one of the two arousability parameters, "natural frequency," can be roughly equated with reactivity, sensitivity, and speed of transmission. Natural frequency determines the frequency of free oscillation following any transient disturbance, and hence it determines the frequency of the EEG "alpha" rhythm (Robinson, 1983).

The second arousability parameter is the "damping ratio" of the system. This can be roughly equated with the duration or persistence of "reverberatory" activity in a closed loop or circuit following the cessation of a stimulus input. To use a simple mechanical analogy, a motor vehicle with good shock absorbers and very little bouncing has a high damping ratio.

The next three chapters show how these fundamental functional parameters relate systematically to temperament differences and to *all* the major dimensions of personality and intelligence that have been indicated by large-scale statistical analyses of individual differences.

6

The Neurological
Determination of Temperament

NATURAL FREQUENCY, EXCITATION-INHIBITION BALANCE, AND THE SANGUINE VERSUS MELANCHOLIC CONTRAST

My findings (Robinson, 1983) indicate that typical global levels of thalamo-cortical activation can be largely accounted for in terms of the values of the two constants that quantify the relative effectiveness of excitation and inhibition and the third constant that quantifies differences in activity levels associated with the influence of external agencies. Since thalamocortical reactivity to stimulation is determined by the reactivity of both excitatory and inhibitory processes, the combination of less effective excitation and more effective inhibition determines lower reactivity of the thalamocortical system of neurons and corresponds to Pavlov's concept of strength. The opposite combination determines greater reactivity and corresponds to Pavlov's concept of weakness. These relationships between excitation, inhibition, and strength or reactivity were not fully understood when my first journal reports were published. As a consequence, the results were taken to signify confirmation of Pavlov's claim, in his final theoretical statement, that while melancholic and sanguine individuals differed in terms of strength, they were also both balanced in terms of excitation and inhibition. In fact, Pavlov's claim concerning differences in strength is supported by the data, but it is now clear that the results do not support

Pavlov's other claim that in melancholic and sanguine individuals, there are balanced processes of excitation and inhibition.

The inverse relationship between excitation and inhibition that determines the strength or *immediate* reactivity of thalamocortical circuits also determines differences in the frequency of "free oscillation" within these circuits or, in technical terms, the natural frequency of the reciprocally connected neurons that constitute the thalamocortical system. Thus, as noted earlier, my data explain the neurological bases of the EEG alpha rhythm but also account for earlier reports that have consistently linked introversion with higher alpha frequencies and extraversion with lower alpha frequencies (Robinson, 1982).

As explained above, natural frequency can be related to Pavlov's strength versus weakness continuum and hence to the data on which his final formulation was based. One can see, however, that Pavlov's strength technique, whether applied using excitatory or inhibitory conditioned stimuli, could not possibly distinguish the separate effects of thalamocortical excitation and inhibition since both are involved in the determination of thalamocortical responsiveness irrespective of the nature of any stimulus. In contrast, my data reveal that for stable extraverts or sanguine individuals, there is predominance of thalamocortical inhibition over thalamocortical excitation whereas the opposite is true for neurotic introverts or melancholics. Thus, sanguine and melancholic individuals, so clearly opposite to each other in general outlook and mood, not to mention other psychological traits, are also opposite in terms of a neurological dimension that can be described in terms of strength, thalamocortical reactivity, or, preferably, natural frequency. They are also opposite to each other in terms of the relative influence of thalamocortical excitation and inhibition, a continuum that is closely aligned with, but not identical to, natural frequency. The clear and unambiguous nature of this relationship is illustrated in Figure 6.1, where a rolling or moving average technique has been employed to plot data obtained from forty-eight human subjects that was first described in earlier publications (Robinson, 1982, 1983).

Here, differences on a sanguine to melancholic continuum of temperament variation are indicated by first standardizing and then summing and restandardizing introversion and neuroticism scores obtained using the Eysenck Personality Questionnaire (EPQ). In the case of melancholic individuals, introversion and neuroticism scores are both high, so that such individuals obtain highest scores on the combined scale. Sanguine individuals obtain lowest scores.

Figure 6.1.

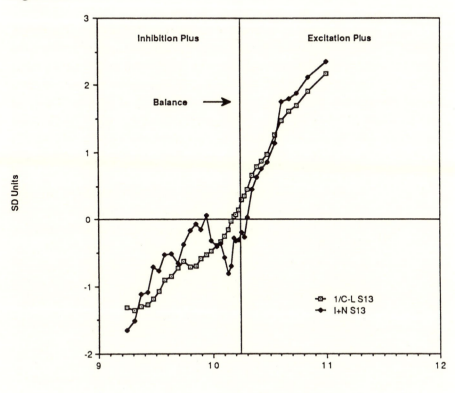

Natural Frequency Hz

The filled squares show sanguine to melancholic differences plotted as a function
of natural frequency. The unfilled squares show excitation-inhibition balance, also
plotted as a function of natural frequency. In both cases, moving or rolling averages
have been used. Here the plotted points *each* represent the averaged data for thirteen
individuals, and this is indicated in the figure by the legend "S13." Moving from
left to right in terms of ascending natural frequency values, one individual is
dropped out and one new individual included to obtain successive points. Exactly
the same procedure is used in all subsequent graphs unless deviations from this
procedure are explicitly noted.

One of the plots in Figure 6.1 illustrates how differences on the sanguine
to melancholic continuum relate to the natural frequency or responsiveness
of thalamocortical circuits. The second plot illustrates the close relationship
between excitation-inhibition balance and natural frequency as well as

showing how excitation-inhibition balance relates to variation along the melancholic to sanguine continuum.

In this theoretical exposition, the rolling average technique is employed to bring out as clearly as possible the nature of empirical relationships and to avoid the distortion that would be introduced by using numerical methods of statistical analysis that are only strictly applicable when a particular form of relationship can be predicted and usually only when the expected relationships are relatively simple. For present purposes it is more useful to explore the exact nature of relationships in the data without any assumptions or preconceptions. However, while this is so, it is noted that when the influence of other neurological variables is discounted, there is a correlation of 0.88 for variation along the sanguine to melancholic continuum and variation of natural frequency. This particular relationship was predicted from the theories of Pavlov and Eysenck, and since it is approximately linear, it is readily quantified in terms of a correlation coefficient. The corresponding coefficient for the temperament continuum and excitation-inhibition balance is even higher, indicating a nearly perfect correlation between these two variables (Robinson, 1982). It can also be seen from the graph that there is an exact balance between excitation and inhibition at a frequency of just over 10.2 Hz, and the transition from the melancholic to sanguine temperament also occurs at this frequency. Although, for the present, it is desirable to evaluate personality differences in terms of the four classical temperaments, it is worth pointing out that when Eysenck's introversion scale is considered on its own, there is also a very close correspondence between changes on this dimension and variation of natural frequency. This is shown in Figure 6.2, where it can be observed that the excitation-inhibition balance dimension and natural frequency are both closely aligned with introversion-extraversion.

Again it is noteworthy that the transition from extraversion to introversion occurs precisely at the point where the relative influence of excitation first exceeds that of inhibition. This fact alone suggests that it is the relative influence of thalamocortical excitation and inhibition that fundamentally determines whether individuals are introverted or extraverted. The corresponding differences in thalamocortical responsiveness due to variation of natural frequency account for the data obtained by Pavlov using the strength technique which contrasted the sanguine and melancholic types.

It will be recalled that Pavlov's first theoretical formulation also contrasted the sanguine and melancholic types, and it has been suggested that the data on which this distinction was based actually indicates that the sanguine type responds more readily to signals of pleasant events than the

Figure 6.2.

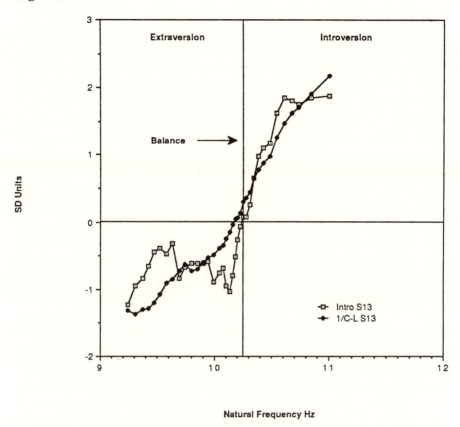

The filled squares show excitation-inhibition balance plotted against natural frequency. The unfilled squares show introversion plotted against natural frequency.

melancholic type. Also, in this context, if nonreinforcement is regarded as
a negative event, Pavlov's findings indicate that the melancholic type
responds more readily to signals of negative events than sanguine individuals. This difference has great theoretical significance since it can account
for the positive mood and optimistic outlook that is characteristic of the
sanguine type while explaining the negative mood and pessimistic outlook
of the melancholic. If sanguine individuals form positive associations more
readily than negative ones, and melancholics learn negative associations
more readily than positive associations, then it is clear that in each case the
world model that is elaborated progressively as a result of learning will be

biased in either a positive or negative fashion and that reference to these world models will bias all judgments and expectations accordingly.

A neurological explanation for the data on which Pavlov's first theoretical formulation was based is also indicated by the results shown in Figure 6.1. These demonstrate that the sanguine and melancholic types differ in terms of the relative influence of thalamocortical excitation and inhibition. In the case of the sanguine type, thalamocortical inhibition is more effective, and this can be related directly to contemporary knowledge of drug effects. As is well known, alcohol, and other drugs used to alleviate anxiety and depression, can all produce a positive shift in mood. It is also now known that alcohol and the minor tranquilizers potentiate the release of an inhibitory neurotransmitter (GABA) in the cerebral cortex.

The most obvious conclusion to draw here is that predominance of thalamocortical inhibition preferentially activates neural systems that give rise to positive affective experience while predominance of excitation preferentially amplifies negative affective experience. This is entirely consistent with the results shown in Figure 6.1, which demonstrate that sanguine types have a *natural* predominance of inhibition whereas melancholic types have a natural predominance of excitation. The drug effects suggest that the mood differences which characterize sanguine and melancholic types are not just epiphenomena of the differences in associative learning noted by Pavlov. It seems likely that the preferential activation of systems mediating negative and positive affective experience not only determines mood differences but also determines differences in the learning of positive and negative associations. Ultimately, of course, the preferential learning of negative or positive associations would be expected to augment the preexisting differences in mood. Confirmation that sanguine individuals do recall and learn positive associations better than negative ones and that melancholic individuals are better able to recall and learn negative as compared with positive associations was sought and obtained in a recent study of human subjects (Robinson and desRosiers, in preparation).

DAMPING RATIO, OVERALL THALAMOCORTICAL AROUSABILITY, AND THE CHOLERIC VERSUS MELANCHOLIC CONTRAST

In addition to the natural frequency or reactivity dimension, excitation and inhibition differences also influence the extent to which activity in thalamocortical circuits can persist after the cessation of a stimulus input. In this case, it is not the difference between excitation and inhibition that is important but the product of the corresponding constants. Variation of this quantity and variation of the constant associated with the influence of the brain-stem arousal system together determine differences in damping ratio. This damping ratio parameter is discussed in greater detail elsewhere (Robinson, 1983), and it will suffice here to note that damping ratio quantifies the tendency for activity to persist in thalamocortical circuits following stimulation.

As noted some thirty years ago by Hebb (1949) when he introduced the concept of cell assemblies, closed neural loops provide a basis for the sustained autonomous brain activity that is necessary to account for some of the most fundamental psychological phenomena. However, a closed circuit alone is not enough to guarantee persistence of activity, since this depends on the degree of damping in such circuits. If the damping ratio exceeds a critical value, then the activity caused by a disturbance will not persist. Below this critical value, activity will persist for longer periods when damping is lower. My results indicate that the damping of thalamo-cortical circuits is usually well below the critical level required for sustained reverberatory activity. The synchronized free oscillation of activity in thalamocortical circuits accounts for the oscillatory character of the EEG, and it is likely that the capacity of such circuits to remain active for extended periods following any disturbance provides the basis for the "engram" or trace required to account for short-term memory.

That possibility is not of immediate interest here, where differences in damping ratio are considered primarily in terms of corresponding differences in general levels of thalamocortical arousability or excitability. To emphasize this relationship, it is noted that with a damping ratio of zero the reverberatory activity caused by any stimulus input would spread to all thalamocortical circuits and continue forever were it not for the fact that the metabolic resources of neurons can be exhausted. Thus, it can be suggested that the uncontrolled discharging of neurons that causes epilepsy occurs when there is zero damping ratio. Anticonvulsant drugs fall into the same general category as tranquilizers, and the former may achieve their effect by increasing damping ratio.

Together, the natural frequency and damping ratio parameters provide a comprehensive description of the dynamic character of the thalamocortical system of neurons, and damping ratio is the second important aspect of thalamocortical arousability already foreshadowed by the earlier analysis of Pavlov's concepts and findings. Recall that extreme differences in strength or natural frequency, which distinguish the sanguine and melancholic types, would be expected to cause corresponding differences in the

degree of inhibition of brain-stem processes. However, the results obtained
by Pavlov using the collision technique suggest that it is the melancholic
and choleric types that differ most in this respect. This implied the existence
of some additional factor in the determination of thalamocortical arousability and in the resultant degree of brain-stem inhibition. That is to say, if
strength differences were the sole determinants of the degree of inhibition
of brain-stem processes, the collision technique should also have contrasted
the melancholic and sanguine types rather than melancholics and cholerics.
It is now clear that damping ratio as well as strength or natural frequency
contributes to *overall* thalamocortical arousability and hence to brain-stem
inhibition. Since natural frequency and damping ratio are both influenced
by the effectiveness of neural excitation and inhibition, the two parameters
are not wholly independent. The manner in which they relate to each other
is shown in Figure 6.3 where natural frequency and damping ratio are both
plotted as a function of natural frequency.

The values used to plot damping ratio differences are actually damping
ratios multiplied by (−1) so that large values indicate greater arousability.
The relationship between the two parameters is important since this determines *overall* differences in thalamocortical arousability. From Figure 6.3,
it is immediately evident that the highest values of natural frequency
correspond to a combination of natural frequency and damping ratio values
that results in highest overall thalamocortical arousability. Thus, in accordance with the interpretation of Pavlov's data proposed earlier, the melancholic type is not only highest in terms of natural frequency, and therefore
weakest in Pavlovian terms, but is also characterized by the highest overall
thalamocortical arousability, and consequently greatest thalamocortical
inhibition of brain-stem processes. This explains why the melancholic type
was found to be extreme in terms of the data obtained using both the strength
and collision techniques. In contrast, the lowest values of natural frequency
correspond to a combination of natural frequency and damping ratio that
indicates middling overall thalamocortical arousability. Thus, as Pavlov's
data suggested, while the sanguine type is lowest in terms of natural
frequency, and therefore strongest, such individuals are not lowest in terms
of overall arousability or in terms of the resultant degree of brain-stem
inhibition. Because this is so, they would not be expected to provide the
most extreme contrast with melancholics when data were obtained using
the collision technique. From Figure 6.3, it can be observed that there is a
zone where there is low arousability due to both natural frequency and
damping ratio. This corresponds to lowest overall arousability, and the
expectation would be that this should correspond to the choleric tempera-

Figure 6.3.

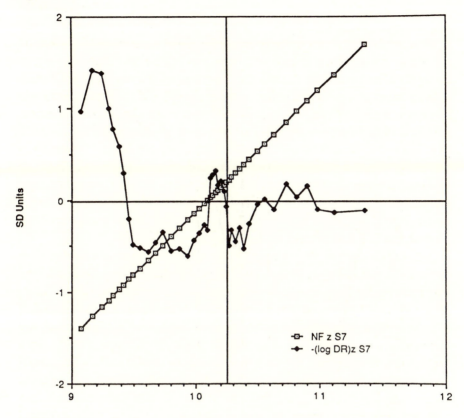

Natural Frequency Hz

The filled squares show damping ratio plotted against natural frequency. For clarity of exposition, low damping ratios, which signify greater arousability, are plotted as large positive values. The unfilled squares show natural frequency plotted against itself so that the relationship between the two different aspects of arousability can be clearly demonstrated. Here the moving averages are based on sets of seven rather than thirteen individuals, and this is indicated in the figure by the legend "S7."

ment and thereby provide the contrast with melancholics suggested by the results obtained using the collision technique.

The differences in overall arousability are brought out more clearly in Figure 6.4 where standardized values for natural frequency and damping ratio have been combined to provide an index of overall thalamocortical

Figure 6.4.

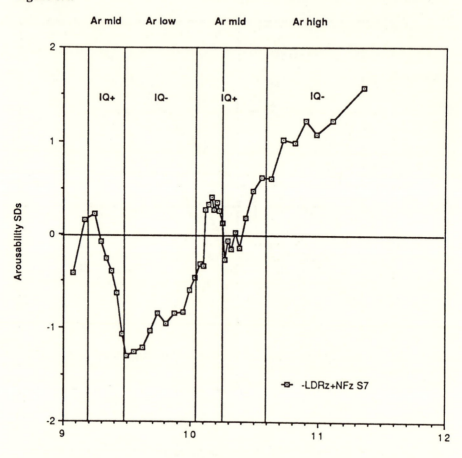

Natural Frequency Hz

Standardized scores for the two aspects of cerebral arousability shown in Figure 6.3 have been summed to obtain an index of *overall* cerebral arousability. This is plotted here as a function of natural frequency. It can be observed that there are two natural frequency zones where there is middling overall arousability and that there are zones of very high and very low arousability. As shown in the figure, zones where highest IQ scores are obtained correspond closely to the zones of middling overall arousability. Lower IQ scores are obtained in the zones where overall cerebral arousability is either high or low. Here the moving averages are based on sets of seven rather than thirteen individuals.

arousability and to illustrate changes in overall arousability as a function of natural frequency.

Figure 6.5 shows introversion and neuroticism scores plotted against natural frequency, and it can be observed that the zone where introversion

Figure 6.5.

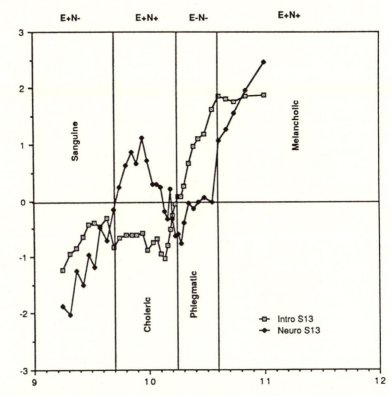

Natural Frequency Hz

The filled squares show variation of neuroticism scores as a function of natural frequency. The unfilled squares show variation of introversion scores, also as a function of natural frequency. The common variance of neuroticism and introversion defines the temperament continuum which contrasts melancholic and sanguine individuals. This contrast relates to the extremes of natural frequency and to the related extremes of excitation-inhibition balance. Notably, the combinations of introversion and neuroticism scores that define the emotionally unstable melancholic and choleric temperaments correspond, respectively, to the natural frequency zones where there is highest and lowest overall cerebral arousability. The stable sanguine and phlegmatic temperaments correspond to the two zones where there is middling overall cerebral arousability.

scores are low and neuroticism scores are high corresponds to the zone of lowest overall thalamocortical arousability shown in Figure 6.4. That is to say, as suggested by the data obtained using Pavlov's collision technique, it is the choleric and not the sanguine type that is lowest in overall thalamocortical arousability and therefore with least inhibition of brain-stem processes. *Thus, it is possible to account for all three of Pavlov's data sets and the corresponding contrasts that provided the basis for his three successive theoretical formulations.*

Pavlov's first formulation contrasted the melancholic and sanguine types in terms of the ease with which responses to signals of pleasant events could be generated and extinguished and, as already mentioned, this can be attributed to differences in the relative influence of thalamocortical excitation and inhibition. The second formulation contrasted the melancholic and choleric types in terms of the data obtained using the collision technique. This can be understood in terms of differences in the degree of *overall* thalamocortical arousability and corresponding differences in the degree of brain-stem inhibition, and it has now been demonstrated that the melancholic and choleric types do indeed fall at the extreme poles of this continuum. Finally, in Pavlov's third formulation, the melancholic and sanguine types are again contrasted, but in this case they differ in terms of strength. Here also, the validity of Pavlov's findings has been confirmed so that it is now possible to provide an integrated neurological explanation for the data underpinning all three of Pavlov's successive theoretical formulations.

THE NEUROLOGICAL BASES OF THE FOUR CLASSICAL TEMPERAMENTS

In Figure 6.6, standardized neuroticism scores are subtracted from standardized introversion scores and the result restandardized to provide a measure of variation on the choleric to phlegmatic continuum. The composite score already used to show variation on the sanguine to melancholic continuum is also plotted. From this it is clear that *the four temperamental types of antiquity correspond to four distinct neurological types indicated by four different natural frequency zones.*

The sanguine and phlegmatic types are extraverted and introverted respectively by virtue of differences in excitation-inhibition balance and notably they do not differ in terms of overall thalamocortical arousability. They are emotionally stable and nonneurotic by virtue of intermediate

Figure 6.6.

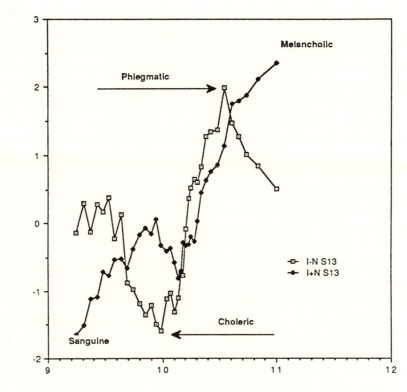

Natural Frequency Hz

The filled squares show variation on the sanguine to melancholic continuum of temperament as a function of natural frequency differences. The unfilled squares show variation on the phlegmatic to choleric continuum as a function of natural frequency. It can again be observed that the four classical temperaments correspond to four distinct natural frequency zones. As already explained, this reflects the twofold influence of differences in excitation-inhibition balance and differences in overall cerebral arousability.

overall thalamocortical arousability and the corresponding intermediate degree of brain-stem inhibition.

The choleric and melancholic types are again extraverted and introverted, respectively, by virtue of differences in excitation-inhibition balance. They are emotionally unstable and neurotic because in the former case thalamocortical arousability is very low with correspondingly reduced inhibition of brain-stem processes. In the latter case, thalamocortical arous-ability is very high with too much inhibition of brain-stem processes.

The sanguine individual is extreme only in terms of predominance of inhibition, and this determines the most characteristic attributes of such individuals. The world is perceived as beautiful and good with correspond-ing feelings of admiration, love, affection, confidence, and optimism.

Phlegmatic individuals are especially notable for their lack of emotional expression. This can be attributed partly to the fact that such individuals are not extreme in terms of either overall thalamocortical arousability or in terms of excitation-inhibition balance and partly to the fact that predomi-nance of excitation, although not excessive, guarantees a more sober, prudent, and generally introverted disposition.

With respect to cholerics, the relatively weak influence of the cerebrum and disinhibition of brain-stem processes can account for strongly ex-pressed emotional reactions that change rapidly as a function of changing circumstances and tend not to persist. Here, emotional instability is associ-ated with poor impulse control. For such individuals, it is difficult to delay gratification, and there is low tolerance of frustration with the possibility of uncontrolled outbursts of rage and aggression when gratification is denied.

In contrast, the emotional instability of melancholics is manifest as undue fear, anxiety, and depression. This can be attributed partly to very high levels of thalamocortical arousability and brain-stem inhibition, where greater sensitivity to stimulation is accompanied by paralysis of action and the undue suppression of impulses motivating the satisfaction of basic biologi-cal needs. The problems of the melancholic are compounded by psycho-logical consequences that derive from extreme predominance of thalamocortical excitation over inhibition. With extreme predominance of excitation, the world is perceived as a dark, ugly, and evil place that evokes loathing, hatred, pessimism, and ultimately despair.

This account of the differences between the four temperament types would not be complete without some reference to levels of activation of the sympathetic division of the autonomic nervous system that are often asso-ciated with differences in emotionality and emotional instability. Psycho-physiologists frequently assess levels of sympathetic activation by measuring palmar skin conductance. This variable was recorded when the EEG data described earlier were obtained and average levels were calcu-lated over the duration of EEG recording sessions.

As shown in Figure 6.7, choleric and phlegmatic individuals differ most in terms of skin conductance, and this provides another contrast between

Figure 6.7.

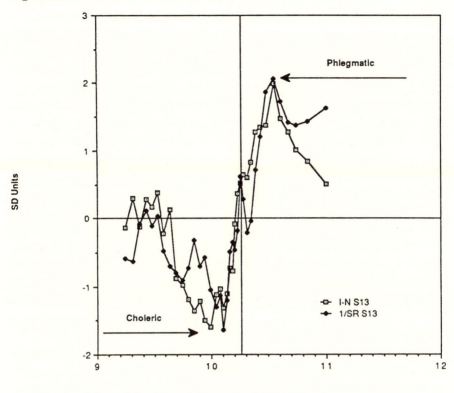

Natural Frequency Hz

The filled squares show variation of palmar skin conductance as a function of differences in natural frequency. The unfilled squares show the corresponding and closely related variation of temperament on the phlegmatic to choleric continuum.

two of the four classical temperaments. The very low level of sympathetic activation associated with choleric individuals can be regarded as relating to lowest overall thalamocortical arousability. The levels indicated for sanguine and phlegmatic individuals can be similarly explained as simply reflecting the degree of thalamocortical arousability. What is surprising is that melancholic individuals do not have the highest levels of sympathetic activation, if this is truly what is measured by palmar skin conductance. The only explanation that can be offered for this departure from theoretical expectations is that very high levels of thalamocortical arousability may inhibit sympathetic activation in a manner analogous to inhibition of the brain-stem arousal system.

TENTATIVE OBSERVATIONS ON THE NATURE OF EMOTIONS

Because the most characteristic emotional responses of melancholic and sanguine individuals can be especially associated with an imbalance of *cerebral* processes and because, as far as is known, they are only evoked when stimuli are processed by the *cerebrum*, it can be suggested that they are not simply secondary derivatives of the "appetitive" and "aggressive" emotional responses that, as Pavlov noted, can still be evoked in decerebrate animals by "unconditioned" stimuli. The very important inference here is that there are "higher" emotions which relate especially to the development and functioning of cerebral processes.

In the first instance, these "cerebral" emotions can be distinguished by virtue of the fact that they do not relate to the satisfaction of basic biological needs and self-preservation. Indeed, the emotions which enable us to experience objects, people, and events as beautiful and good or, alternatively, as ugly and evil, have frequently resulted in the supreme sacrifice of life itself.

We do not learn emotions. We learn to perceive patterns of associations, and somehow particular patterns trigger particular emotional experiences. It seems that there is a "preparedness" to respond to highly complex patterns of learned associations with emotional reactions that are qualitatively different from those associated with the simple and more elementary "unconditioned" stimuli.

This view of things constitutes a more general application of the idea proposed by Seligman (1971) to account for phobias, but here the fear response does not necessarily require a prior association between the feared object and some unpleasant experience. It is suggested that when particular patterns of activity occur in the CNS, and this would be determined by the opportunity to learn and by the learning process, then innately determined emotional experiences are triggered. These transcend the mere denotation of similarities and differences to endow what is experienced with the power to motivate behavior, and in a way that preserves what is good for humanity in general, while rejecting what is bad. This conception of the nature of "cerebral" emotions or those unlocked or triggered *directly* by *learned* stimulus patterns, or patterns of associations, can be related to Jung's conclusions concerning the existence of archetypes and the existence of a collective unconscious.

The positive or negative character of cerebral emotions can only be attributed to evolutionary development. This means that moral behavior must be determined by the particular character of emotional responses evoked by life experiences. Thus, in general, the attitudes and behavior of people with respect to other people, society, and their whole environment will be determined by the actions of these other people and of society as well as by the intrinsic neurological differences that account for temperament variation and emotional or moral bias. People, society, and the environment may evoke feelings of love and affection in particular individuals, and if so, they will be cherished and protected. In other individuals, the same people, society, and environment may evoke feelings of hatred and disgust, and if so, they will be despised and rejected.

Consideration of the neurological differences associated with the different temperament types indicates that the positive and negative character of the "higher" emotions attending moral behavior is in some sense related to the preferential activation of cerebral excitatory and inhibitory processes. Under normal circumstances, this must be influenced in some manner by the character of particular stimulus inputs. However, in the case of sanguine individuals, predominance of inhibition enhances the positive cerebral emotions, whereas for melancholics, predominance of excitation enhances negative cerebral emotions. The moral disposition of the sanguine and melancholic types can be characterized as "loving God" and "hating the Devil," respectively. In contrast to these two types, the choleric individual is dominated by more primitive emotions that reflect less cerebral influence over brain-stem processes and relate more to self-preservation and the satisfaction of basic biological needs. There is least emotional or moral bias in the case of the phlegmatic type, but such individuals have a moral disposition akin to that of melancholics in tone if not degree.

The findings reviewed here greatly extend Pavlov's research in that it is possible to provide a comprehensive neurological explanation for all four classical temperaments. This subsumes Pavlov's major findings and is based on the direct measurement of thalamocortical activity. In addition, it is possible to explain the major dimensions of personality and intelligence variation that have been revealed by contemporary large-scale statistical analyses of individual differences. It is to these that I now turn.

7

The Neurological Determination of Contemporary Personality Dimensions

INTROVERSION-EXTRAVERSION

The Neurology of Introversion-Extraversion

Figure 6.2 shows that introversion-extraversion scores are closely related to differences in the relative influence of thalamocortical excitation and inhibition that covary with differences in natural frequency. Since natural frequency is one aspect of arousability, there are theoretical grounds for expecting a relationship between this variable and introversion-extraversion (Eysenck, 1967). However, there is some indication that excitation-inhibition balance is also a fundamental cause of these personality differences. This conclusion is greatly reinforced when Figure 6.4 is compared with Figure 6.5. This comparison clearly indicates that when changes in overall arousability and changes in excitation-inhibition balance are positively correlated, which is true for the upper half of the natural frequency range, there is also a high correlation between these variables and introversion-extraversion. In the lower half of the natural frequency range, there is a more complex curvilinear relationship between overall arousability and excitation-inhibition balance. In this region, the introversion-extraversion scores vary in a way that indicates sensitivity to changes in *both* overall arousability and excitation-inhibition balance. More specifically, in the natural frequency zone that corresponds to stable extraversion, there is middling overall arousability, and here extraversion can *only* be explained by reference to predominance of inhibition over excitation. In contrast, the extraversion scores in the choleric zone appear to be amplified by very low overall arousability.

Thus, although introversion-extraversion scores are influenced by thalamocortical arousability, arousability is clearly not the only cause of such differences. It would appear that *introversion-extraversion differences are caused by differences in overall arousability and by differences in excitation-inhibition balance, but it is only in extraverted groups that the separate effects of these two neurological dimensions become evident.*

Introversion-Extraversion and Overall Thalamocortical Arousability

Overall thalamocortical arousability differences, and resultant differences in the degree of cerebral inhibition of brain-stem processes, explain a contrast between impulsivity and behavioral inhibition that constitutes one of the fundamental dimensions of personality. Barratt (1985) has done the most to map out the precise nature of this important and ubiquitous dimension, but impulsivity is also known to be one of the two major "components" that constitute a broader introversion-extraversion dimension (Robinson, 1986a). The theory being elaborated in this account suggests that the relative influence of cerebral and brain-stem processes would also cause other less obvious but equally important psychological differences. These would include "introverted" and "extraverted" mental orientations or attitudes akin to those described by Jung (1971), as well as differences in the relative performance of "verbal" and "spatial" tasks. Further discussion of the neurological mechanisms responsible for these mental or cognitive differences will be reserved for the next chapter. Here it is sufficient to state that the psychological differences deriving from variations in overall thalamocortical arousability are most easily summarized by reference to the contrast between melancholics or neurotic introverts and cholerics or neurotic extraverts. More specifically, it is the manner in which these two temperaments are opposed to each other that is important.

Introversion-Extraversion and Excitation-Inhibition Balance

As noted earlier in this discussion, differences in the relative influence of cerebral excitation and cerebral inhibition also determine differences on the EPQ introversion-extraversion scale. This second neurological dimension can be related to the trait of "sociability" that, like "impulsivity," has been identified as a major component of a broadly conceived introversion-extraversion dimension. Here again, the findings and related theoretical developments detailed in this account suggest that differences in sociability are not the only or even the most fundamental effects caused by differences in the relative influence of cerebral excitation and inhibition. Indeed, sociability differences can now be seen as just one aspect of differences in behavior that result from bias in the learning of "positive" and "negative" associations and from corresponding differences in cognitive performance and in "optimism" versus "pessimism." As noted earlier, these differences can also be related to moral bias and to the contrast between "loving God" and "hating the Devil." This contrast serves to illustrate the profound and complex nature of the psychological consequences of neurological heterogeneity. Again, the simplest way to sum up the psychological differences of interest is to point to temperament differences and in this case to the manner in which melancholics or neurotic introverts are opposed to sanguine individuals or nonneurotic extraverts.

The Dual Nature of the Extraversion Problem

From the foregoing it is evident that the manner in which cerebral parameters relate to each other determines the structure and organization of personality differences already suggested in a vague and inexact manner by statistical analysis but not previously understood or explained. Not surprisingly, failure to understand the meaning of these structural differences has given rise to much debate, and, as Eysenck notes (Robinson, 1986a), one of the two questions most frequently asked in the domain of personality research concerns the dual nature of extraversion. This question has now been answered because two neurological dimensions have been identified that might both contribute to general "approach" and "avoidance" behavioral tendencies and to a psychological dimension of introversion-extraversion conceived in the broadest possible terms. The difficulty with this dimension is that the underlying neurological determinants are only aligned or only act in concert in the domain of introversion. Thus, although high introversion scores always relate to the same set of specific psychological traits, and to the same underlying neurology, this is not true in the case of extraversion scores. High extraversion scores can signify *either* predominance of cerebral inhibition over excitation *or* low overall thalamocortical arousability. As we have seen, the psychological consequences of these two conditions are fundamentally different even if they might conceivably result in some superficially similar approach behaviors.

It is especially noteworthy that the difficulties arising for those who seek to determine personality structure using analytical statistical techniques are precisely those encountered by Pavlov when confronted by findings that could not be accommodated by a simple unidimensional theory. The "duality of extraversion" problem relates to the same underlying organization of neurological parameters. The correlation between traits of sociability and impulsiveness reflects the fact that melancholics or people with high introversion scores are extreme on the two corresponding neurological dimensions. This correlation is only of the order of 0.5 because the opposite poles of the two neurological dimensions do not coincide and they actually determine the two very different personality profiles of sanguine and choleric individuals. Since the correlation only reflects constraints imposed by the structure of neurological variables and, more specifically, coincidence of two determining variables that would have different psychological effects, there is no basis for suggesting that impulsivity and sociability have anything in common, or that they are in any sense equivalent, except insofar as they might both cause superficially similar approach and avoidance tendencies.

Since, as we shall see, neuroticism is especially related to differences in overall arousability, one can also explain Eysenck's observation that very high introversion scores are almost invariably associated with elevated neuroticism scores, whereas both high and low neuroticism can be found in association with extreme extraversion scores. As discussed earlier, the same underlying relationship between overall thalamocortical arousability and excitation-inhibition balance accounts for Pavlov's finding that the melancholic type was extreme in terms of the results obtained using *both* the collision and strength techniques but in the former case there was a contrast with cholerics whereas in the latter case the contrast was provided by the sanguine type.

NEUROTICISM

The Neurology of Neuroticism

Turning now to the neuroticism dimension, Figure 6.5 illustrates that as for introversion-extraversion, the lowest and highest neuroticism scores are associated with the extremes of natural frequency and of excitation-inhibition balance. This accounts for periodic reports of a correlation between these two personality variables and clearly relates to the "independence of E and N" problem that, according to Eysenck, is the other question that arises most frequently in the domain of personality measurement. In fact, despite all efforts to do so, it has been impossible to construct introversion-extraversion and neuroticism or emotionality scales that are wholly independent of each other (Robinson, 1986a). From Figure 6.5 we can see now that high negative correlations must always be obtained between E and N scores in any group made up of sanguine and melancholic individuals, or even when a majority of persons belong to these categories. In groups of introverts, melancholics, or dysthymic neurotics one must also expect high negative correlations between E and N scores. All of these expectations follow from the manner in which the E and N scales relate to the underlying neurological dimensions. Clearly, the independence problem is no longer a problem when, as now, these relationships are understood.

Comparing Figures 6.4 and 6.5, one can see how the neuroticism dimension differs from introversion-extraversion, thereby defining the choleric and phlegmatic temperaments. *High neuroticism scores occur when there is either very high or very low overall thalamocortical arousability. Low neuroticism scores occur in those natural frequency zones where there is middling overall arousability.*

Although the difference between the E and N dimensions is readily apparent in Figure 6.5, it is also obvious that neuroticism relates to the same cerebral parameters that determine EPQ introversion-extraversion and not especially, as Eysenck (H. J. Eysenck and S. B. G. Eysenck, 1976; H. J. Eysenck and M. W. Eysenck, 1985) has hypothesized, to the limbic system or to the sympathetic division of the autonomic nervous system.

The Psychological Significance of Neuroticism Scores

The coincidence of high neuroticism with high or low cerebral arousability is entirely consistent with Eysenck's conception of neuroticism as indicating predisposition to neurotic breakdown, because it is only to be expected that psychological problems will occur when the cerebrum is close to the extreme limits of its operational range and is therefore less able to sustain normal psychological functions. More specifically, one can see that differences in overall thalamocortical arousability determine the relative balance or imbalance of cerebral and brain-stem processes. Very high or very low thalamocortical arousability determines too much or too little cerebral control of brain-stem processes and this results in the kind of psychological conflicts that Freud came to regard as the sine qua non of mental illness. Here it is important to note a departure from Freudian theory in that such conflicts are explained in this account as mere symptoms of the underlying imbalance of cerebral and brain-stem processes and they have no primary causal significance.

The conflicts referred to just now are not the same for melancholic and choleric individuals, where there is predominance of cerebral and brain-stem processes, respectively. The former can be linked to *internal* conflict and to exceptionally strong inhibition of more "primitive" and "selfish" behaviors associated with the satisfaction of basic biological needs. Where brain-stem processes are dominant or less strongly inhibited, there is *external* conflict between the individual and society. Because there is inadequate control of brain-stem processes the individuals in question act impulsively, are unable to delay gratification, and, if frustrated, are also less able to inhibit rage and aggression.

It will be recalled also that it was the very high and very low arousability types, namely melancholics and cholerics, in which Pavlov was able to induce experimental neuroses using the collision technique. With Pavlov's collision technique, his experimental animals were required to make increasingly difficult discriminations until they reached the limits of their ability to perform such tasks. One can suggest that thereafter, the nature of responses was not determined by the character of the stimulus input but only by the degree of brain-stem inhibition.

It can be suggested that with predominance of the cerebrum, and a very high level of brain-stem inhibition, the effect of stress would be to further increase this inhibition so that melancholic animals simply stopped responding to all stimuli whatever their significance. With predominance of brain-stem processes, and a very low level of brain-stem inhibition, the effect of stress would be to further increase brain-stem activation so that choleric animals lost the capacity to inhibit responses.

The fact that these "neurotic" breakdowns were associated with a lesser ability to make discriminations can be related to data obtained from human subjects which indicate that very high and very low overall arousability is associated with lower IQ scores (Robinson, 1989, 1991; Robinson, Gabriel, and Katchan, 1994). The relationship between thalamocortical arousability and IQ is shown in Figure 6.4. The implication here is that predisposition to neurotic breakdown is not just a function of arousal-related learning disorders and emotional instability, but also results partly from arousal-related perceptual and cognitive deficiencies with a correspondingly reduced ability to cope.

Melancholic and choleric individuals are very different and actually opposite to each other in terms of some of the most fundamental psychological variables. However, there is the common denominator that all such individuals are poorly adjusted, discontented, and unhappy. At this level of abstraction, it is possible to conceive of a unitary psychological dimension that relates meaningfully to the EPQ N scale or to other comparable scales. Thus, although the N scale can be regarded as a good indicator of neurotic predisposition and mental instability, and although there is a valid conceptual basis for such a dimension, there is also clearly a problem in that high scores are ambiguous and cannot be properly interpreted without reference to introversion-extraversion scores. This is true for both the neurological and psychological domains, and as a result different investigators attempting to study "neuroticism" could quite easily arrive at exactly opposite conclusions.

It appears from the data discussed here that N and E are both primarily and fundamentally determined by differences in cerebral function. However, consistent with Eysenck's theory, it is also possible that high N may be related to activation of the sympathetic division of the autonomic nervous system *whatever the magnitude of E scores*. This possibility follows from an important theoretical distinction that must be made between "cerebral arousal" and "cerebral arousability" (Robinson, Gabriel, and Katchan, 1994, pp. 145–148). The first term, cerebral arousal, refers only to the *state* of cerebral activity at any particular time and irrespective of the source or cause of this activity: It could be due to either the physicochemical properties of cerebral tissue or to projections from the brain-stem arousal system following activation by external stimulation.

The second term, cerebral arousability, refers to the *intrinsic* properties of cerebral processes that, all else equal, might be expected to correlate positively with cerebral arousal. However, all else is not equal because low cerebral arousability will result in less cerebrally mediated inhibition of the brain-stem reticular formation. In turn, *disinhibition of this structure must cause greater brain-stem mediated cortical activation or arousal*. Thus, neurotic extraverts with lowest cerebral arousability could sometimes experience high levels of cortical arousal and perhaps also correspondingly high levels of limbic and sympathetic activation. This brain-stem mediated cerebral arousal would depend crucially on the degree of brain-stem stimulation provided by the external environment. In this way it is possible to suggest that high N scores, whether for extraverts or introverts, may always be associated with greater sympathetic activation. Finally, there is a valuable theoretical bonus here because the environmental dependency of cerebral arousal in choleric or neurotic extraverts can account for the legendary "changeability" of extraverts, or more correctly, of extraverts with high neuroticism scores.

Turning now to the pathological effects of very high or very low arousability, a useful analogy is that of blood pressure. Here also there is a range of variation within the general population that is considered normal. Beyond the limits of normal variation, there are disorders of increasing severity with the progressive appearance of a variety of discrete symptoms not evident in normal individuals. This conception of predisposing biological factors in the aetiology of mental illness is most lucidly and convincingly argued by Claridge (1995).

The concept is particularly useful in that chronic differences in thalamo-cortical arousability, like blood pressure, are not necessarily due to genetic differences but may be caused by neural disease processes, brain damage, and probably also by chronic stress or even isolated traumatic experiences. This, of course, would explain why a range of different "organic" disorders give rise to similar symptoms and why the symptoms of organic disorders are often similar to those used to define "functional" disorders. Just as the general state of health of the cardiovascular system is indicated by a simple index of blood pressure, so the general state of health of the CNS might equally well be evaluated by a reliable and valid index of overall thalamo-cortical arousability.

Finally, in this account of neuroticism, it is important to emphasize that mental illness is not just conceived in terms of the *primary* consequences of extremely high or low thalamocortical arousability. Important secondary consequences would be expected because of the cumulative pathological effect of a disordered learning process. As we shall see momentarily, it is also possible that high levels of damping may cause psychopathology even when overall arousability is not extreme.

PSYCHOTICISM

As well as the extraversion (E) and neuroticism (N) scales that can be related to the four classical temperaments, the Eysencks have also developed a psychoticism (P) scale and a scale to measure dissimulation, the lie (L) scale. Although at this stage less well researched or developed, these scales also appear to relate to an important and fundamental dimension of personality variation that can be identified in the work of different investigators (Eysenck and Eysenck, 1985). In the general population, high P scores appear to signify a psychopathic-like personality profile (Eysenck and Eysenck, 1976). However, while convenient as a summary description, this nomenclature should not be taken to imply that all the related traits and attributes are negative ones.

From Figure 7.1, it is clear that the P scale is especially related to differences in damping ratio. The implication here is that abnormally high levels of damping may relate to actual psychopathy while normal variation within the general population determines a major dimension of personality which contrasts a range of attitudes and behavioral dispositions that can be broadly described as prosocial versus antisocial. As might be expected from earlier discussion of the temperament types, the lowest P scores coincide with the natural frequency zone associated with the sanguine temperament,

Figure 7.1.

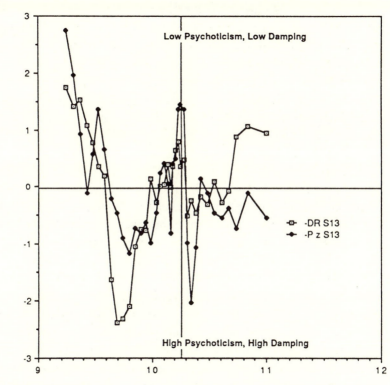

Natural Frequency Hz

Filled squares show variation of psychoticism scores as a function of natural frequency. The unfilled squares show corresponding and related changes in damping ratio. Note that the standardized psychoticism scores and damping ratios are both multiplied by (-1) to ensure that, as elsewhere, higher values always signify greater arousability.

and high P scores coincide with the zone associated with a choleric disposition. However, the highest P scores are obtained by some but not all
individuals in the natural frequency zone associated with the phlegmatic
temperament.

It transpires that the "phlegmatic" individuals with high P (and low L)
scores have E and N scores that are only marginally lower than average and
in this respect they are not typical of the phlegmatic type. The individuals
concerned are closest to the point of excitation-inhibition balance at around
10.25 Hz and, as we shall see momentarily, form one of three very high IQ
groups. The high IQ scores of this particular subgroup contrast with the
lower IQ scores that are associated with cholerics, and, as already noted,
the E and N scores also differ. It might be suggested that, in this high IQ
subgroup, high P scores signify something other than a psychopathic-like
personality profile, but independent data concerning the lifestyles, attitudes,
and preferences of such individuals indicate otherwise. The fact that highest
P scores are obtained by a particular high IQ group accounts for the
empirical observation that there is usually a small positive correlation
between P and IQ (Eysenck and Eysenck, 1976).

One of the strengths, but also one of the weaknesses, of conventional
intelligence measures is that they are designed to minimize the influence of
culture. As a result, they are not the best instruments for assessing important
aspects of learning ability. Since this is so, it is quite possible that individuals
with a reduced capacity to learn the complex associations that are necessary
for the acquisition of social and cultural knowledge may yet obtain high IQ
scores if they have other perceptual and cognitive strengths.

Recall that with greater damping the activity in neural circuits tends not
to persist and it is also likely that the lateral spread of activity would be
restricted. In Pavlovian terms, the cortical activity caused by any input
would be "concentrated" in time and space, and it is likely that the corresponding associations in long-term memory would be similarly restricted.
That is to say, high levels of damping would be expected to prevent the
integration of experience that is necessary for the development of complex
abstract concepts.

The same concentration of neural activity can account for Witkin's
important concept of "field independence" and the "differentiated" cognitive style that is indicated by superior performance on cognitive tasks where
it is necessary to distinguish simple geometric shapes embedded in complex
patterns. Individuals in the high IQ subgroup that obtain the highest P scores
also obtain remarkably high field-independence scores on Witkin's Embedded Figures Test, and, as we shall see in the next chapter, they perform

exceptionally well on the "performance" as distinct from "verbal" subtests of the Wechsler Adult Intelligence Scale (WAIS).

GRAY'S THEORY OF ANXIETY

The results summarized in Figures 6.4 and 6.5 have a bearing on Gray's (1982) "alternative" to Eysenck's arousability theory, and this chapter would be incomplete without some reference to Gray's contribution. The empirical basis for Gray's model is provided by the results of experiments on rodents, but it owes much to Eysenck's concepts since it is only through reference to these that Gray's findings can be related to human individual differences.

Gray stresses the importance of an "anxiety" dimension with neurotic introverts at one pole and nonneurotic extraverts at the other. This contrasts the melancholic and sanguine types and is congruent with findings summarized here but described in detail elsewhere (Robinson, 1982). According to Gray, this dimension can be attributed to individual differences in the operation of the septohippocampal system but, as we have seen, direct measurement of brain electrical activity in humans shows unequivocally that the melancholic or anxious temperament relates to higher levels of activity in the cerebrum as a whole and not just to functional characteristics of the septohippocampal system (Robinson, 1982). Here it is important to emphasize that we are not dealing with conflicting claims or theories but rather with a conflict between Gray's theory and unambiguous empirical findings which demonstrate directly that melancholics have high cerebral arousability.

An obvious weakness of theories of human behavior that are based on rodent studies is that rat brains differ greatly from human brains. In the case of Gray's research, there is the less obvious problem that he does not actually study individual differences or psychological traits. That is to say, the rats studied in psychology experiments are genetically homogeneous and therefore cannot exhibit individual differences comparable to those of human subjects. Equally important, the changes in brain activity brought about by Gray's experimental manipulations are comparable to "state" differences *within* individuals rather than to "trait" differences *between* individuals.

A more detailed discussion of Gray's model and related problems is provided elsewhere (Robinson, 1986b). Here I will only add that Gray is not alone in pointing to the psychological significance of the septohippocampal system. In fact the septohippocampal system has been linked to a plethora of psychological effects which, in the absence of any detailed specification of functional characteristics and the manner in which they produce particular psychological effects, leads only to the theoretically empty conclusion that when the structural and functional integrity of the CNS is violated, we may expect complex and varied psychological consequences. One must also bear in mind that the relatively large number of rodent septohippocampal studies do not necessarily indicate any special importance or significance of this system but may, to a large extent, reflect the relative ease with which it can be studied in rats. In this respect, rodent septohippocampal studies are not unlike the ever-popular fruit fly studies of geneticists.

REAL PERSONALITY DIFFERENCES VERSUS DESCRIPTIVE COORDINATES

The only reliable and useful measures of personality differences have been developed with the aid of statistical techniques that analyze correlations between pairs of questionnaire items (Eysenck and Eysenck, 1985). However, statistical procedures alone cannot yield valid scales (Eysenck, 1992). The relative success of the Eysencks' system of personality description can be attributed in part to the fact that they have always resisted the temptation to publish scales purporting to measure a multiplicity of traits. Instead, the Eysencks concentrated on the relatively small number of broad replicable dimensions that give rise to scales with high reliability coefficients.

Another important consideration would appear to be the use of criterion groups of neurotics to establish the original E and N dimensions, rather than relying solely on the statistical analysis of questionnaire data as most others have done. With hindsight one can see that this approach ensured that the Eysencks' dimensions relate in a very simple and direct manner to real personality differences and to the four classical temperament types that are everywhere evident and, in terms of their basic features, easy to identify.

Although it is now clear that the Eysencks' scales provide an effective and comprehensive means of describing the fundamental personality and temperament variations caused by individual differences in brain function, it is also clear that they are best considered a system of Cartesian coordinates. What this means is that scores on all of the scales or coordinates must be known in order to uniquely specify or describe any actual personality or any meaningful personality differences; just as latitude and longitude must be known in order to uniquely specify any geographical location. Consequently, to say that someone has a high E score turns out to be no more useful than to state that a particular geographic location is to be found at a latitude of 55 degrees.

The E and N coordinates are all that are necessary to identify the four temperament types, and it has now been demonstrated that the psychological significance of differences in cerebral arousability is also most easily understood in terms of just four temperament types. The question arises, where does the P dimension fit in? This third coordinate obviously suggests the possibility of additional temperament types, but recall that the P, E, and N dimensions are all explicable in terms of just two arousability parameters. Thus, although it is useful and interesting to distinguish and measure the specific traits and attributes subsumed under the P dimension, it is also evident that this cuts across the personality space already defined by E and N. That is to say, the P dimension contrasts neurotic extraverts and stable introverts, whose damping ratios tend to be high, with neurotic introverts and stable extraverts, whose damping ratios tend to be low. Thus, although we obtain a different perspective with the P scale, and although there are important and interesting new psychological contrasts, the scale does not appear to identify any personality types additional to those already associated with the different combinations of E and N.

Another way to think about this important issue is to enumerate the four quadrants of the two-dimensional personality space defined by the E and N dimensions. When this is done we can contrast quadrants one and two (E+) with quadrants three and four (E–). Similarly, quadrants two and three (N+) can be contrasted with quadrants four and one (N–). With no additional quadrants or dimensions needed, we can contrast quadrants two and four (P+) with quadrants one and three (P–).

It might appear from the foregoing that the P dimension is redundant. This is only true in the limited sense that P is not needed to place people in one of the four temperament categories. Against this, one can assert that P greatly adds to the descriptive power of the Eysencks' system and provides important additional information about the psychological consequences of neurological differences. Here one must also be mindful of the fact that the Eysenckian system is almost unique in its reference to a biologically based theoretical framework and to criterion groups. This has undoubtedly helped to align the Eysencks' factors or coordinates with the real neurological variables that determine temperament differences. We have seen that E is especially associated with the natural frequency parameter (although also influenced by overall cerebral arousability), and the significance of the P scale is further demonstrated if one recalls the data linking P and the damping ratio. *Thus, E and P relate in a simple and direct manner to the two arousability parameters.* In contrast, N relates to the neurological variables in a more complex manner. There is a curvilinear relationship with the composite overall arousability parameter such that *high N scores coincide with the two extremes of overall cerebral arousability.* As noted, there is the possibility of a simpler linear relationship between N and cerebral *arousal* (as distinct from arousability), but the validity or otherwise of this suggestion must be determined by future study.

Eysenck has always warned of the limitations of factor-analytic procedures used to analyze questionnaire-item correlations, and advised against interpretation of scores on individual scales without reference to the other scales. In his 1982 book, *A Model for Personality*, he points out that the final factors obtained from such analyses never completely escape the shadow of the initial selection of items or tests, or the selection of methods of extraction or rotation. He emphasizes that it is only by reference to measures external to the factor-analytic tautology, but linked with theories concerning the causation of personality factors, that we can break the *circulus vitiosus*. Yet the literature clearly shows that many researchers have not followed this advice. In some personality studies, investigators have examined the difference between high scorers and low scorers on the EPQ E scale in order to gain insights concerning the nature of the extraversion dimension. However, all such exercises are doomed because, as we have seen, high extraversion scores can signify two quite different psychological profiles with different causal agencies operating at the neurological level. The same is true for high neuroticism scores. Unfortunately the results of such studies have accumulated in the literature so that much confusion exists concerning the correlates and possible causes of personality differences. This is especially so with respect to earlier attempts to obtain information concerning the biological bases of such differences.

One last issue should be mentioned. There has been a long-sustained debate between H. J. Eysenck, R. B. Cattell, J. P. Guilford, and others concerning the "correct" number of factors that should be "extracted" using factor-analytic procedures. Eysenck has held to the "orthogonal" factor-analytic procedure favored by most statisticians because it extracts independent or uncorrelated factors. Cattell has been a forceful advocate of the "oblique" procedure, which allows correlated or overlapping factors.

The approaches of Cattell and Eysenck are also dissimilar in other respects. For example, Eysenck first hypothesized the existence of a neuroticism or emotionality dimension and proceeded to examine how neurotics differ from the general population. Thus he could immediately benefit from reference to criterion groups, but he could also anticipate that these groups would reveal the most important and fundamental dimensions of personality in their most exaggerated and easily observed manifestations. Notably Eysenck's first factor, and to a large extent each subsequent factor, was conceived and introduced on the basis of theoretical and empirical considerations that had little to do with factor analysis. It is certainly true that factor analysis was eventually used to help sort out the most suitable questionnaire items for evaluation of N differences and ultimately also to ensure maximum independence of N, E, and P items. However, there was no attempt here to determine factors, or the number of factors, just from statistical analyses.

In contrast, Cattell sought to ascertain all possible personality factors from an analysis of words in the English language that relate to personality. Cattell, unlike Eysenck, relied heavily on the results of his statistical analyses in order to ascertain both the existence of factors and the number of such factors. In this endeavor, the use of the oblique factoring procedure was justified by the assertion that real personality factors are unlikely to be entirely independent and uncorrelated. By using a set of questionnaire items that could be traced back to a lexicon of personality words, Cattell could argue that his factors covered the whole personality domain described by the English language. Since Cattell also allowed his factors to be correlated, it is easy to appreciate how he ended up with more factors than Eysenck.

Finally, and again unlike Eysenck, Cattell sought to make his whole endeavor as atheoretical as possible. Claiming greater objectivity, he relied heavily on his statistical procedures to determine putative dimensions of personality. Various other statistical procedures were utilized to determine the "correct" total number of factors to extract from his data. As is well known, he eventually arrived at a system of sixteen "first-order" correlated factors. These reduce to about eight "second order" factors if the correlations between the original factor scores are submitted to a second factor analysis.

Despite Cattell's claims to the contrary, there is no objective procedure that can specify some definite number of factors in any given data set. These factoring procedures operate like Occam's razor since they will extract an infinite number of factors that account for progressively smaller and smaller amounts of the total variance of the original variables. Reference to the size of "eigenvalues," or to the "statistical significance of the last residual," or to the so-called scree test, do not provide any information about the "correct" number of factors. These are all arbitrary criteria that only reflect preexisting subjective judgements about the amount of variance a factor should explain before we deem it worthy of consideration.

One may criticize Cattell's "specialist" approach if only because the important questions and issues in a complex subject like psychology cannot be resolved by a "bottom up" strategy that relies too much on data from a single source. As for behaviorism, claims of objectivity and "scientific purity" obscure an abrogation of responsibility for the intellectual effort that is needed to integrate information from many sources in order to generate the theories needed to guide and direct data collection. The important point, however, is that despite Cattell's very different approach, he ultimately identifies two second-order factors, "exvia versus invia" and "emotionality," that are very similar to the extraversion and neuroticism factors of the EPQ. The same core dimensions emerge time after time in virtually all studies of personality traits. Unfortunately, this consensus rapidly melts away if one goes beyond the E, N, and P dimensions of the Eysenckian system (Eysenck, 1985). It seems that in descriptive personality systems, one may choose to have a small number of independent and reproducible factors and corresponding measuring scales with very high reliabilities or else a larger number of correlated factors that are much less easily reproduced and scales with appreciably lower reliabilities. The general rule seems to be that as the number of scales increases, their reliabilities decrease, and one can be much less certain about the corresponding "factor structure."

From a researcher's viewpoint, it is better to have a smaller number of reliable scales or coordinates, but it is recognized that those involved professionally in personality description might opt for a system that specifies a larger number of specific attributes. Also, when we get down to pinpointing actual personality types, it is possible that one might have equal success with a small number of very reliable coordinates or a large number that are less reliable. In this account, it would be wrong to deny that the Eysenckian system is considered superior to that of Cattell and Guilford. However, it is also important to acknowledge that Cattell and Guilford have made great contributions to the development of a science of personality measurement, both in terms of long-continued systematic research and in terms of important original contributions to the development of methods and theory.

Eysenck, Cattell, and Guilford all belong to the pioneering generation of psychologists who invented many of the statistical procedures used by today's researchers. Today we have a new generation of "factorists" weaned on SPSS and other "user-friendly" computer programs that take the hard work and intellectual effort out of statistical analysis. The results are unfortunate since the real progress in personality measurement that was made in the 40s, 50s, 60s and 70s is now endangered by worthless articles that bring the whole science of personality measurement into disrepute. The "great idea" that now enthralls many factorists is that there are five personality dimensions, usually referred to as the "five factor model" or "the big five" (Costa and McCrae, 1985; Digman and Inouye, 1986; Goldberg, 1990, 1993; Hogan, 1986; Trapnell and Wiggins, 1990; Norman, 1963). Arguments against any notion that it is possible to specify a particular number of dimensions have already been detailed, but it is worth mentioning some of Eysenck's (1992) comments in his response to an article by Costa and McCrae (1992). Eysenck argues against the notion that there are five basic factors. Among other important considerations, he points to the lack of any nomological network or theoretical underpinning for the five factors and notes that there is failure to suggest any biological link between the genetic causation of such factors and their behavioral expression.

Although the so-called big-five model is currently being promoted with some vigor, it seems to be little more than a convenient number that falls opportunistically between three and eight. One can only be pessimistic concerning research on personality if theories are to be replaced by advertising slogans. Cattell (1995) is rightfully scathing in his criticism of the big five factorists. Referring to an article by Goldberg (1993), he describes it as "a piece of free-flowing writing appealing to those untrained in 'state-of-the-art' multivariate experimental psychology [but] it would take a lifetime to unravel the subjectivity and errors of factor analysis in the noisy street demonstration of psychologists which he [Goldberg] assembles (207)." After detailing various errors of omission and commission, Cattell (1995) notes that "the results of rotations or non-rotations among the five factor enthusiasts gives a dense jungle of mutually incompatible solutions (208)," and it does seem clear that *they are not even describing the same five factors.*

From the neurological evidence considered earlier, it is now evident that one could never hope to specify the actual organization or structure of personality differences with certainty without knowledge of the causal agencies involved. The Eysenck scales and all other comparable scales developed with the aid of factor analysis must inevitably confound effects related to the different but overlapping causal agencies identified in this account.

There is also the problem that particular traits such as "approach" versus "avoidance" tendencies or "happiness" versus "unhappiness" may be determined by more than one causal agency. We have seen how the resulting mismatch between real personality dimensions and statistical factors gave rise to the "duality of extraversion" problem and to the "independence of E and N" problem. The value of the empirical findings described here, and the power of the related theory, is most convincingly demonstrated when it is possible to resolve quite specific issues of this nature that have been a source of controversy in the literature on personality for over half a century.

For the future, it is suggested that the contrasts provided by the different temperament types should become the main focus of interest in personality research since these relate to the real and most fundamental personality differences. Melancholics and cholerics fall at the extreme poles of overall thalamocortical arousability. Melancholics and sanguine individuals fall at the extreme poles of imbalance between cerebral processes of excitation and inhibition, but they also fall at the extremes of natural frequency. Finally, there is the contrast between sanguine and phlegmatic individuals that relates to extremes of damping ratio.

It is appropriate now to consider the neurological determination of intelligence differences, and we shall see that this also determines relationships between personality and intelligence dimensions. Ultimately this gives rise to the first truly comprehensive and detailed account of brain, mind, and behavior relationships and of human individual differences.

8

The Neurological Determination of Intelligence Dimensions

Research on EEG-intelligence relations was carried on as an extension of earlier work, which led to the discovery of theoretically meaningful relationships between personality dimensions, temperament differences, and the neurological parameters described in preceding chapters (Haier, Robinson, Braden, and Williams, 1984; Robinson, 1982, 1983, 1986a, b, 1987; Robinson, Haier, Braden, and Krengel, 1984a). In the course of this earlier work, I was led to suppose that cortical arousability should also relate to intelligence.

The term cortical arousability refers to a characteristic or typical level of activation of thalamocortical neurons that is determined by the general availability and balance of excitatory and inhibitory neurotransmitter substances. In general terms, it was thought that differences in thalamocortical arousability might be a crucial neurological factor that can limit the amount of information available to an individual and thereby determine differences in general intelligence. In particular, it was hypothesized that intelligence-test performance and arousability are related in a curvilinear fashion analogous to the Yerkes-Dodson law (Yerkes and Dodson, 1908; see also Broadhurst, 1959). Thus, across individuals, intelligence-test performance would be optimal when there is an intermediate degree of arousability. For progressively higher or lower degrees of arousability, there would be correspondingly lower intelligence scores.

Of course, the general notion of a link between intelligence and arous-ability is not new. To account for the effects of brain damage on intelligence-test performance, Hebb (1949) was forced to invent an arousal mechanism, the "cell assembly." According to Hebb, contemporary theories of behavior were inadequate since they did not account for some of the most fundamental psychological facts. Classical SR learning theory failed to allow for any autonomy of brain function and for related psychological facts such as selective attention. Field theory, on the other hand, tried to account for perception without reference to learning. Through the mechanism of the cell assembly, Hebb's theory was able to relate learning and perception while at the same time providing a basis for the autonomous brain activity or arousal that is necessary to account for behavior such as selective attention.

A decade later, Hebb (1959) refers to the gaps in neurological knowledge that existed when his theory was formulated and suggests that "the greatest omission of all is of course the brain-stem arousal system of Moruzzi and Magoun (1949) whose fundamental role in all higher processes is now clear. No account of intellectual processes and their relation to the brain can be taken seriously today when this is omitted from the reckoning (Hebb, 1959, pp. 266–267)." Hebb goes on to suggest that an intermediate degree of arousal might be optimal for cognitive processing.

The psychological significance of brain-arousal mechanisms has been considered in detail by Samuels (1959) and also by Magoun (1963). Both of these authors make the point that arousal mechanisms can modify cortical activity partially or globally, and consequently they have the capacity to regulate the content of conscious experience with all that this entails.

AROUSABILITY AS THE DETERMINANT OF EEG AND IQ CORRELATIONS

In the publications referred to above, both Samuels and Magoun review evidence which demonstrates conclusively that the activity of the arousal systems, as noted earlier, can be observed in EEG recordings. It follows directly that EEG measures relate to arousability and that there should be a relationship between such measures and intelligence-test performance.

In fact, there is a considerable literature on the relationship of EEG "spontaneous" and "evoked" potentials and intelligence which shows many significant but apparently inconsistent correlations (Haier, Robinson, Braden, and Williams, 1984; Vernon, 1993; Vogel and Broverman, 1964). However, I have found that this confused and confusing literature can be rendered comprehensible if reference is made to the "inverted-U" hypothesis of the relationship between arousability and intelligence. For the most part, studies of EEG and intelligence have not been guided by either theoretical expectations concerning the particular EEG variables which should relate to intelligence or by any expectation of the form such relationships should take (Robinson, 1993). In practice, the results have often been evaluated in terms of rectilinear correlation coefficients which, by default, only test the validity of a simple rectilinear model. It follows that, in a representative sample, the proposed curvilinear inverted-U relationship would not be detected. However, significant positive or negative rectilinear correlation coefficients could be obtained in unrepresentative groups if the individuals concerned were either low on arousability or high on arousability, respectively.

In the earlier EEG studies, carried out prior to 1965, there are remarkably consistent reports of a positive relationship between the frequency of spontaneous EEG activity and intelligence in low arousability groups. That is to say, in groups of elderly people, children, or mentally retarded persons.

In recent times, technological advances have allowed the recording of EEG responses to specific stimuli, often a light flash or tone. Since 1965, as many as nineteen studies have investigated the possibility of a relationship between these evoked potentials and intelligence. Despite great variation of conditions and procedures, most studies did find some evidence of a relationship between intelligence and differences in evoked potential waveforms. Most of the correlations have been small, but again there is some indication that the strongest evidence of a simple rectilinear relationship is to be found in low arousal groups.

The last point mentioned is well illustrated by Hendrickson's (1982) study of 219 London schoolchildren where a negative correlation coefficient of 0.83 was obtained between full-scale WAIS IQ and a composite evoked-potential measure. In two published studies and one as yet unpublished study carried out using similar evoked-potential procedures, my results suggest that Hendrickson's findings do not generalize to adults in the middle years of the life-span (Haier, Robinson, Braden, and Williams, 1983; Robinson, Haier, Braden, and Krengel, 1984b). However, significant correlations ranging up to 0.69 were found in three different samples composed of individuals in their late teens or early twenties. Evidence of a simple linear relationship was also found in a group of elderly subjects. Moreover, when behavioral criteria were employed to select out elderly individuals closest to the sleep threshold, there was an appreciable increase in the magnitude of the correlations. These results led to the conviction that

a simple linear model is inadequate, and suggested that serious consideration be given to the arousability hypothesis.

AROUSABILITY, INFORMATION PROCESSING, AND
INTELLIGENCE FACTORS

Robinson (1989, 1991) has described how the two arousability parameters, natural frequency and damping ratio, relate to WAIS IQ scores. In this
analysis of data from forty-eight adult subjects, it was found that the highest
IQ scores do indeed coincide with middling overall arousability defined in
terms of the relative contributions due to natural frequency and damping
ratio. That is to say, there is a strong relationship between IQ and arousability across individuals which is analogous to the inverted-U curve that has
frequently been used to describe the relationship between performance and
arousal within individuals.

Figure 6.4 illustrates in general terms how IQ varies as a function of
overall arousability. From the total of forty-eight, all but one of seventeen
individuals with WAIS IQ scores greater than 130 fall in the two middling
arousability zones shown in the figure.

Figure 8.1 illustrates the relationship between full-scale WAIS IQ and
natural frequency considered in isolation. A logarithmic transformation has
been performed on the natural-frequency values to ensure a more symmet-
rical distribution. The plotted values were again obtained using a rolling or
moving average technique. Each point represents the average of six IQ
scores and the corresponding average for natural-frequency values. The
point on the extreme left of the graph was obtained by calculating averages
for individuals with the six lowest natural-frequency values. The next point
was obtained by dropping out the three participants with lowest natural-frequency values and including three new individuals with the next highest
natural-frequency values. This procedure was applied across the whole
range of natural-frequency values, moving to successively higher but
overlapping sets of values. Again the merit of this procedure is that it
demonstrates the exact form of the empirical relationship between natural
frequency and IQ in a clear-cut and unambiguous manner. The standard
errors for the highest and lowest means are shown, and it can be observed
that these are very small as compared with differences in the means that are
a function of differences in natural frequency. With one exception, all
seventeen individuals with IQs greater than 130 fall in the two high IQ zones
denoted A and B in the figure. When account is taken of differences in

Figure 8.1.

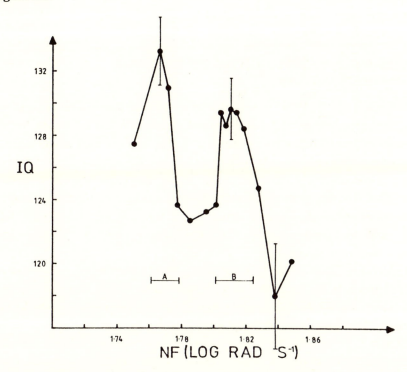

Moving averages for natural frequency, expressed as log radians s⁻¹, plotted against corresponding IQ averages. Standard errors are shown for high and low IQ groups. All but one of seventeen individuals with IQs greater than 130 fall in the two natural-frequency zones denoted "A" and "B." In this case, and in Figure 8.2 that follows, the moving averages derive from successive sets of six individuals where each new set is obtained by dropping out the three persons with lowest natural-frequency values and including three new individuals with the next highest natural-frequency values. This figure is reproduced with permission from the *International Journal of Neuroscience*, 1989, 46, p. 218.

damping ratio, these high IQ zones correspond to the zones of middling overall arousability shown in Figure 6.4.

To illustrate the combined influence of natural frequency and damping ratio, rolling averages for damping ratio were calculated in the same way as for the IQ averages. In Figure 8.2 the damping ratio and IQ averages are both plotted as a function of differences in natural frequency. Inspection of the superimposed curves shows how the IQ/natural frequency relationship is influenced by variation of damping ratio. On the left side of Figure 8.2, where arousability due to natural frequency is lower, it can be observed that

Figure 8.2.

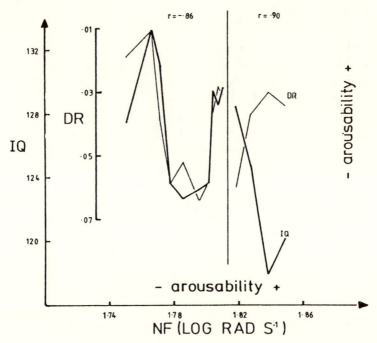

Graphs for IQ/natural frequency and damping ratio/natural frequency are superimposed. Where natural frequency is lower, there is a negative relationship between the damping ratio and IQ means (r = -0.86). Where natural frequency is higher, the relationship between damping ratio and IQ means is positive (r = 0.90). This figure is reproduced with permission from the *International Journal of Neuroscience*, 1989, 46, p. 219.

greater arousability due to lower damping ratios is associated with higher IQ and vice versa. In other words, when lower arousability due to natural frequency is compensated by higher arousability due to damping ratio there is higher IQ. A sharp transition, indicated by the vertical line, occurs near the middle of the graph. To the right of this line, the relationship between damping ratio and IQ is reversed. In this part of the figure, arousability due to natural frequency is high. Where damping ratio further increases arousability, IQ is reduced. Where arousability due to damping ratio is low, and compensates for high arousability due to natural frequency, there is higher IQ. The strong association between the IQ and damping-ratio means is quantified in terms of the correlation coefficients shown to the left and right of the vertical line. It is clear from these results that IQ is very strongly influenced by natural frequency and damping ratio and that the highest IQ scores occur when there is an intermediate degree of overall arousability.

These results have profound theoretical significance since the relationship between arousability and intelligence can be explained in terms of the way in which differences in thalamocortical arousability influence the acquisition, retention, and utilization of information. At the same time, it is possible to discern the neurological bases for the general intelligence factor described by Spearman (1927) and for a bipolar ability factor that was frequently encountered in the early factor analytic studies reviewed by Burt (1949). In terms of arousability theory and related findings, it is also possible to account for a reported relationship between this bipolar factor and the introversion-extraversion dimension of personality.

An intermediate degree of thalamocortical arousability is conceived as optimal for information processing because of the way in which thalamocortical arousal influences the following systems or processes.

1. The neurological system of information transmission
2. The neurological system regulating attention and recall
3. The neurological process of learning

Arousability and Information Transmission

An intermediate degree of cortical arousability should be optimal for information transmission because, as far as is known, all information received by the brain is transmitted centrally by variation of neural firing rates. This is also true for all information transmission within the brain. Since all physical systems including neurons have a limited operating range with upper and lower limits determined by physical constraints, it is clear that very high or very low levels of "background" activation or arousal will limit the variability of neural firing rates and hence limit the amount of information that can be transmitted. The brain receives much information by virtue of the contrasts provided by differential rates of firing of different neurons. These contrasts would be attenuated by high or low levels of arousal. Thus, while all aspects of information processing would be impaired by deviation from middling arousability, it can be suggested that a specific psychological effect would be a reduced capacity to make discriminations.

This accords with Spearman's (1904) interpretation of his early findings when he claimed that a single general function would suffice to account for practically all the correlations he observed between different ability measures. He identified this "fundamental general function" with the elementary process of "discrimination" and provided empirical support for the earlier ideas of Sully and Bain who both asserted that the discernment of difference is the most fundamental element in all intellectual activity (Burt, 1949). The fundamental importance of discriminative capacity is further suggested by recent findings reported by Lynn, Wilson, and Gault (1989), which show that the capacity to discriminate simple auditory tones is highly correlated with scores obtained on the WAIS. Similar findings have been obtained by me in a study not yet published.

More generally, it is well known that at the extremes of very high or very low levels of arousal, whether due to traumatic experiences, sleep, or drug effects, the psychological correlate of reduced information transmission is a total loss of discriminative power and unconsciousness.

Arousability, Attention, and Recall

An intermediate degree of thalamocortical arousability should be optimal for information processing because it is optimal for the regulation of attention and recall and for the operation of "working memory." This follows from the premise that the content of conscious experience alters as a function of differences in the degree of thalamocortical arousability and resultant differences in the degree to which there is inhibition of the brain-stem reticular activating system. The latter system provides background cortical activation that is necessary for perception to occur (Samuels, 1959). With higher intrinsic thalamocortical arousability, there is a correspondingly higher level of thalamocortical activity or arousal and stronger inhibition of brain-stem processes necessary for perception. While the overall effect of thalamocortical processes on the brain stem is known to be inhibitory, it is suggested that this inhibition is selective and graded in a manner which causes greater inhibition of familiar stimulus inputs when these do not signal positive or negative consequences.

In effect, learned and selective inhibition of brain-stem processes is regarded as the mechanism which determines the psychological phenomenon of habituation, and this is consistent with the fact that neurons of the brain-stem reticular activating system are most easily activated by novel stimuli. If, as suggested, inhibition of the brain stem is selective and graded, it follows that a generally higher degree of thalamocortical arousability, and correspondingly higher levels of cortical activation, will increase the number of brain-stem elements that are inactivated and thereby reduce the range of stimuli that can be perceived. This ensures that when there is high cortical arousability, there can only be a selective and serial mode of perceiving and representing the external environment.

At the same time, however, high intrinsic thalamocortical arousability must result in lower thresholds for the evocation of memories and ideation that is unrelated or less closely related to contemporary stimulus inputs than would otherwise be expected. The greater blocking of external inputs, which includes proprioception and other internal sources of stimulation, together with lower thresholds for memories and ideation, determines an introverted mental orientation which effectively limits the range of information that can be accessed, and determines a particular mode of information processing. The capacity of working memory is also reduced since the ability to "keep something in mind" will be impaired by irrelevant and distracting ideation.

In contrast, with low intrinsic thalamocortical arousability, the threshold for evocation of memories and ideation would be high so this kind of mental content is reduced. At the same time, low thalamocortical arousability results in weaker inhibition of the brain-stem reticular activating system. This will result in less blocking and selection of stimulus inputs, and in an attendant change in the character of cortical activity that, in turn, determines a change in mental content. This change is such that mental content will relate more to the external environment and to a wider range of parallel sensory inputs. Again, it is emphasized that "external" signfies external to the CNS and does not exclude somatic inputs. In this case, the "broadband" and less selective perception of external inputs, together with higher thresholds for the evocation of ideation, determines an extraverted mental orientation. Again, the range of information that can be accessed is reduced, and again the capacity of working memory is reduced, since the ability to keep something in mind is impaired by irrelevant and distracting external stimuli.

Clearly, an intermediate degree of arousability is in this case also optimal because transient shifts in arousal state will allow both internal and external sources of information to be accessed as necessary and, in addition, this information can be better utilized in problem-solving activities, since the capacity of working memory is effectively increased when the distraction due to both irrelevant ideation and irrelevant external stimuli can be minimized.

Although attention has not always been defined in the same way, tests of the ability to concentrate attention have long been included in measures of general intelligence, and some have had high loadings on general intelligence factors when these are extracted as the principal component in a battery of tests. So much so that before the concept of general intelligence became less fashionable, various writers including Wundt suggested an identity with the "capacity for attention" (Burt, 1949).

When middling arousability is contrasted with both high and low arousability, it is to be expected that those individuals with middling arousability will do better on tasks which involve keeping something in mind while executing related cognitive operations, as in oral arithmetic problems, and in tasks requiring a working memory of large capacity. It is only in this sense that the capacity to concentrate attention would be associated with a general intelligence factor.

If such a factor was extracted as the principal component in a set of tests, and an orthogonal factor was subsequently extracted, one would expect this to contrast individuals high and low on arousability. In terms of cognitive abilities, one would expect a bipolar factor contrasting a selective, idea-driven, and serial mode of attention deployment with a relatively unselective, stimulus-driven and parallel mode of attention deployment. In fact, as Burt points out, when this method of factor analysis was more commonly employed, such a bipolar factor was frequently encountered. Burt (1949, pp. 197–198) describes the contrast in terms of "fixating" as opposed to "diffusive" attention. Notably, he also pointed out that the same factor contrasted differences in perseveration, emotionality, objectivity, and introversion-extraversion. This is precisely what would be predicted from arousability theory.

The effects of high and low arousability on the regulation of attention and recall have already been described in terms of introverted and extraverted mental orientations; but as described in previous chapters, there is an actual and strong relationship between the arousability parameters described here and the introversion-extraversion dimension of personality (Robinson, 1982, 1987). Arousability theory explains this relationship and also accounts for the earlier findings described by Burt as well as accounting for the structural relationship between principal components or general intelligence factors and orthogonal bipolar factors.

Arousability and Learning

An intermediate degree of thalamocortical arousability should be optimal for information processing because it facilitates the development of a more valid world model through associative learning. In the first instance, this follows from the statements already made concerning information transmission and the regulation of attention and recall which specify optimal conditions for information processing prior to the occurrence of learning and the forming of associations.

The general advantage of enhanced information transmission and discriminative power is self-evident, but the way in which the regulation of attention would influence associative learning is not immediately obvious and must therefore be described in some detail. Clearly, the kinds of associations that are learned will depend on the manner in which attention is deployed. An introverted mental orientation will favor the learning of associations between discrete features of the external environment that are attended to selectively, in serial fashion, and in a way that is driven by ideation. This mode of learning favors the acquisition of cultural knowledge through language since language consists of circumscribed stimulus events that are arranged in serial fashion. Moreover, since learning is selective and driven by ideation, it is likely that any new learning will relate to the extension and development of existing ideas.

In contrast, an extraverted mental orientation, due to low thalamocortical arousability and weak inhibition of the brain-stem reticular activating system, will favor the learning of associations among many parallel stimulus inputs. In this case, the progression of learning in time is determined to a far greater extent by the nature of unfolding events and is much less influenced by ideation. Moreover, because there is an association of many parallel inputs through different sensory modalities, this mode of learning favors the acquisition of knowledge concerning spatial and kinesthetic relations which enhances all practical abilities involving physical interaction with the material environment.

In addition to these effects on learning, it can also be suggested that thalamocortical arousability has a direct influence on the development or selective facilitation of neural connections that is logically necessary to account for associative learning. This proposition is described in greater detail elsewhere (Robinson, 1989). Here it is sufficient to state that high chronic levels of cortical activation would be expected to have an effect on learning analogous to repetition or strong stimulation. Both high and low thalamocortical arousability will cause a high level of cortical activation. In the first case because intrinsic arousability is high. In the second case because low intrinsic arousability results in disinhibition of the brain-stem reticular activating system and correspondingly high levels of externally mediated cortical arousal. Thus, as well as the preselection of two broad categories of inputs that can be associated, it may be argued that high and low arousability will ensure that within these categories associations are formed too easily and unselectively.

This would be advantageous in terms of "rote" learning and for the acquisition of special abilities of a reproductive character. However, it would be disadvantageous insofar as associations within the introverted and extraverted domains, or more specifically the melancholic and choleric domains, would tend to have equal strength. A good world model should reflect the frequency with which events coincide so that in conditions of uncertainty, there is a basis for discriminating associations that reflect chance coincidence from those that relate to frequently experienced coincidences and hence acquire the status of a relation.

If learning occurs too easily, then all associations will tend to have equal weight or strength, and there is no basis for discriminating valid relations from chance coincidence. On the other hand, if learning occurs with too much difficulty, many relations will go unrecognized. A useful analogy here is the type I and type II errors of formal statistical inference. However, it should also be noted that, in the nature of things, elementary relations are experienced more frequently than complex ones. Thus, when learning occurs too readily, there would be a reduced capacity to distinguish elementary relations within complex ones. In contrast, when learning occurs with too much difficulty, there should be a reduced capacity to perceive complex relations. In this way it can be argued that for associative learning, and especially for the development of a superior relational world model, middling arousability should be optimal. At this higher relational level, the effect of middling arousability would be manifest as the enhanced capacity to educe relations and correlates that eventually became a central feature of Spearman's (1927) conception of general intelligence.

Again, reference can be made to those earlier factor-analytic studies reviewed by Burt (1949), where it was common to extract a principal component or general intelligence factor first, and then subsequently to extract an orthogonal factor. Burt points out that in

most researches in the cognitive field, the factor which accounts for the greater part of the individual variance, after the first or general factor has been removed, is a bipolar factor distinguishing verbal from non-verbal abilities. It appears with group tests and with individual tests, with psychological examinations and educational examinations, with Binet tests in the schoolroom and with tests of recruits for all the fighting services. It tends to divide both children and adults into verbal (or "intellectual") and non-verbal (or "practical") groups. (184)

Once more it can be suggested that this factorial structure can be explained by arousability theory and that the bipolar factor again reflects a contrast between high and low arousability and the two different categories of associations that are preselected by the introverted and extraverted modes of attention deployment. Relevant studies of my own do show that introverts and extraverts have different WAIS profiles such that introverts do better on the verbal subtests and extraverts do better on the performance subtests (Robinson, 1985, 1986c). Also, as noted earlier, there is a strong relationship between introversion-extraversion and thalamocortical arousability. Finally, from arousability theory it can be suggested that the bipolar factor relates to reproductive as distinct from eductive abilities.

NEUROLOGICAL DIFFERENCES DETERMINING THREE DISTINCT HIGH IQ TYPES

Without any contradiction of the finding that middling arousability determines high IQ, further analysis of the data described by Robinson (1989) reveals that high IQ scores are associated with three distinct combinations of the natural frequency, damping ratio, and excitation-inhibition balance parameters. That is to say, middling arousability can be achieved by different combinations of the neurological parameters, and all of these combinations are associated with high IQ scores. Data which illustrate this observation are shown in Table 8.1. To avoid any confusion, it is noted that high natural frequencies indicate high arousability whereas low damping ratios indicate high arousability. Also, it is noted that a zero value for the balance parameter, described here as "delta," indicates a balance between thalamocortical excitatory and inhibitory processes.

It is remarkable that in the sample of forty-eight individuals, described by Robinson (1989), all but one of the seventeen subjects with IQ scores greater than 130 fall into the three quite distinct neurological categories shown in Table 8.1. The first two categories can be distinguished in terms of all three neurological parameters with no overlap in the distributions. In the first category, natural frequencies, damping ratios, and delta values are all higher when compared with the corresponding values for the second group. In the third category, natural frequencies and delta values do not overlap with those of the second category, and the damping ratios do not overlap with those of the first category.

Although high and low, respectively, on the three neurological parameters, the first two groups are similar in that there is a strong positive correlation between natural frequency and damping ratio. Indeed, the combined data for these two groups yield a highly significant product-moment correlation coefficient ($r = 0.81$). Thus, in these two categories, variation of arousability due to natural frequency is offset by corresponding but opposite changes in arousability due to damping ratio. This constancy

Table 8.1
Means and Standard Deviations for Neurological Parameters, Personality Scores, and Intelligence Test Scores in Three Different Neurological Categories

	Category 1	Category 2	Category 3
WAIS IQ	136.8(5.7)	137.1(3.2)	134.4(2.2)
Natural Freq.	64.9(0.88)	59.2(1.34)	64.8(1.23)
Damping Ratio	0.073(0.036)	0.027(0.022)	0.016(0.008)
E-1 Balance	0.027(0.017)	-0.050(0.017)	0.004(0.007)
Extraversion	10.4(0.95)	13.9(5.81)	11.5(7.86)
Neuroticism	10.9(0.63)	8.2(2.46)	10.0(7.85)
Psychoticism	9.4(4.57)	3.3(1.70)	4.4(3.31)
Lie	1.3(0.96)	3.4(1.97)	4.2(3.17)
Information	0.49(0.66)	0.87(0.32)	0.85(0.41)
Comprehension	0.33(0.70)	0.40(0.81)	0.64(0.41)
Vocabulary	0.30(0.35)	0.93(0.21)	0.63(0.46)
Similarities	0.29(0.57)	0.40(0.35)	0.98(0.18)
P. Arrangement	0.72(0.74)	0.62(0.91)	-0.17(0.50)
B. Design	0.97(0.34)	0.57(0.66)	0.54(0.68)
Object Assy.	0.79(0.27)	0.32(0.90)	0.43(0.27)
Pict. Comp.	0.39(1.18)	0.20(0.74)	0.74(0.33)
Arithmetic	0.69(0.77)	1.13(0.40)	0.09(0.70)
Digit Symbol	0.76(0.93)	0.95(0.57)	0.39(0.69)
Digit Span	0.60(1.02)	0.67(0.93)	0.89(0.54)
N	4	7	5

of thalamocortical arousability is reflected by remarkably similar personality profiles, especially in the first category.

In the third category, a nearly perfect negative correlation was found between natural frequency and damping ratio ($r = -0.99$). In this group, the negative correlation derives from the constraint that IQ is enhanced by excitation-inhibition balance and the covariation of the excitation-inhibition constants that is necessary to maintain balance results in a negative relationship between natural frequency and damping ratio. The result is that balance only guarantees high IQ within a limited range of covariation of the excitation-inhibition constants. Outside this limited range, arousability due to natural frequency and damping ratio is either too high or too low, and balance alone is no longer enough to sustain high IQ.

With respect to IQ scores, it appears that within a certain range, changes in arousability can be tolerated more than is usually the case provided that there is an exact balance between excitation and inhibition. The same cannot be said for personality characteristics since there are large changes in extraversion (E) and neuroticism (N) as measured by the Eysenck Personality Questionnaire (Eysenck and Eysenck, 1975).

In Table 8.1, the patterns of mean WAIS subtest scores vary across the three categories in a way that suggests some relationship with the three main factors normally revealed by factor analysis of WAIS subtest scores. More generally, the patterns suggest that the three categories can be related meaningfully to the three major factors described by Cattell and Horn as "fluid" and "crystallized" intelligence and as "short-term memory and retrieval" (Cattell, 1971, 1987). The first four WAIS verbal subtests are considered markers for crystallized intelligence. The next group of performance tests are considered markers for fluid intelligence. Arithmetic and Digit Span, in the last group of three subtests, are markers for Cattell's short-term memory and retrieval factor. The differences in subtest means across the three categories suggest that the first category can be aligned with fluid intelligence, the second with short-term memory and retrieval, and the third with crystallized intelligence.

One would not expect an exact correspondence between the ranking of category subtest means and loadings on intelligence factors. The profiles for categories two and three are similar in that higher scores were obtained on verbal as distinct from performance subtests. Factor analysis would almost certainly represent covariation of subtest scores related to these two categories in terms of a single "verbal" or "crystallized intelligence" factor with any residual variance assigned to a less important "attention-concentration," "freedom from distractibility," or "short-term memory and retrieval" factor.

When account is taken of this consideration, the relationship between categories and factors is greatly clarified while at the same time a serious limitation of the factor-analytic procedure is thrown into sharp relief. That is to say, factor analysis is blind to the influence of different agencies causing variation of test scores if these agencies are responsible for covariation of scores on the same set of tests. In the present case, different causal agencies are responsible for covariation of distinct but overlapping sets of tests. The operation of different causal agencies would influence any factor solution, but there would be no one-to-one correspondence between the factors obtained and the causal agencies determining test variance. As already noted, the covariance of the overlapping subset of tests would tend to be represented by a single factor which would confound the influence of different causal agencies. The extent of any overlap would determine the degree of distortion, but such distortion should be reduced if the factor-analytic procedure allows correlated factors. Notably, Cattell has insisted that correlated factors have greater psychological relevance, and, although this can now be disputed, it is clear that correlated factors could reveal structural features that would not be observed if only a principal component and orthogonal factors were extracted as described earlier. Taking account of the previous discussion of principal components and orthogonal factors, one is drawn to conclude that different factor-analytic procedures reveal different aspects of structure and that these must all be accounted for in any comprehensive theory of intelligence.

In this account, a detailed analysis of subtest differences will not be presented, but it is worth noting that even within a relatively small and highly selected data set, and with minimal variation of IQ, the three neurological parameters determine statistically significant differences in some WAIS subtest scores. This, of course, is why the three categories have different WAIS profiles. In particular, high scores on the Similarities subtest, which is the best marker for the third category, relate to low values of damping ratio ($t = 2.20$, df 15, $p < 0.05$) and high values of natural frequency ($t = 2.57$, df 15, $p < 0.05$). Block Design and Picture Arrangement are both good markers for the first category. High scores on Block Design relate to high damping ratios ($t = 2.33$, df 15, $p < 0.05$), and the same is true for Picture Arrangement ($t = 2.29$, df 15, $p < 0.05$). Finally, Arithmetic and Vocabulary are both good markers for the second category. High scores on Arithmetic relate to low values of natural frequency ($t = 2.83$, df 15, $p < 0.05$) as do high scores on Vocabulary ($t = 2.94$, df 15, $p < 0.05$). The difference between the Similarities and Picture Arrangement subtest scores proves to be particularly sensitive to variation of damping ratio. With a median split on damping ratio, there is no overlapping of the corresponding distributions of the difference variable. Thus, even when overall arousability is relatively invariant, high damping is associated with better performance on the Picture Arrangement subtest and relatively poor performance on Similarities. The converse is true for low damping. Notably, these particular subtests are considered the best WAIS markers for fluid and crystallized intelligence, respectively, which suggests that among high IQ subjects with middling overall arousability, the fluid versus crystallized distinction relates mainly to variation of damping ratio.

High damping relates to fluid intelligence whereas low damping relates to crystallized intelligence. Insofar as there is a "verbal" versus "performance" distinction here, the effect of variation in damping appears to mimic the effect of variation in overall arousability. This may be due to the fact that high damping would restrict the lateral spread of cortical activity and thereby restrict the development and accessing of ideation. Low damping would favor the development and accessing of ideation, which would account for better verbal performance. In this case, however, owing to middling overall arousability, it is likely that verbal performance is eductive in character as distinct from the reproductive verbal abilities associated with low overall arousability. If this were indeed the case, then it is possible that the terms fluid and crystallized intelligence have misleading connotations. Also, if the fluid versus crystallized distinction depends on the relative involvement of ideation and better integrated neural activity, it is to be expected that as learning proceeds during the course of the life-span, the progressive and experience-related integration of neural elements will ensure enhanced access to ideation and correspondingly improved verbal abilities but with a decline in performance on those tasks commonly associated with fluid intelligence.

The actual age-related decline in performance of fluid ability tests has frequently been associated with degeneration of neural tissue. Here it is suggested that such a decline is to be expected as a function of learning. That is to say, when the experience-related integration of neural elements proceeds beyond a certain point, individuals should become less able to perceive parts or elements and better able to perceive integrated Gestalt patterns. This accords with the data shown in Table 8.1, where the category associated with fluid intelligence is characterized by very high scores on the EPQ P scale and very low L scores. This particular combination indicates a psychopathic-like personality profile that can be explained by an analytical, as distinct from wholistic, mode of perception and by a restricted access to ideation.

It is emphasized that individuals in the three different neurological categories perform at an above average level on virtually all of the WAIS subtests, and this is due to middling overall arousability. The different WAIS profiles in the three categories are clearly related to the particular way in which middling arousability is achieved, with some WAIS subtests relating more strongly to one or other of the three neurological parameters. Notably, these effects are distinct from the WAIS profile differences mentioned earlier, which do relate to differences in overall arousability.

CONCLUSION

Middling arousability is optimal for the development of high IQ; and consistent with theoretical expectations, there are clear indications that high and low arousability relate, respectively, to special aptitudes for the performance of some verbal and some manipulative visuospatial tasks, with the individuals concerned also differing on the introversion-extraversion dimension of personality. It is suggested that these arousability-related special aptitudes relate to the bipolar verbal/educational versus spatial/mechanical factor described in earlier factor-analytic studies. The merit of this proposal is that the special aptitudes are aligned with a dimension of arousability that is effectively orthogonal to the contrast between middling arousability and both high and low arousability that accounts for the general intelligence factor. Since the method of factor analysis employed in earlier studies was constrained to seek out precisely this kind of structure in any data set, there is good reason to assume that these early factor-analytic solutions would reflect the twofold influence of arousability differences described above.

Additional insights were obtained from an analysis of the data from high IQ subjects. It transpires that high IQ subjects fall into three distinct neurological categories with corresponding differences on the major dimensions of personality and WAIS profiles. These categories can be meaningfully related to the fluid intelligence, crystallized intelligence, and short-term memory and retrieval factors described by Cattell and Horn, although an exact correspondence would not be expected owing to limitations of the factor-analytic technique. It was suggested that the method of factor analysis favored by Cattell and Horn, which involves rotation to simple structure and allows oblique or correlated factors, would be best able to discriminate psychological differences associated with the different neurological types. Thus it can be argued that different factor-analytic procedures reveal different but complementary aspects of the structure of intelligence.

In this chapter, we have seen how fundamental dimensions of neurological variation determine the structure of intelligence and how, with this new knowledge, it is possible to reconcile earlier notions of intelligence structure based mainly on the statistical analysis of test data. No less important, there is support for a description of intelligence in terms of "the availability of information," and it has been possible to specify in precise terms just how the more fundamental neurological differences can influence different neurological processes mediating the acquisition, retention, and utilization of information.

In preceding chapters, it was possible to map out in a clear and unambiguous manner the neurological determinants of the major dimensions of personality and to show, after more than two millennia, the validity of the ancient fourfold classification of temperaments. Finally, it has been possible to demonstrate how intelligence differences relate to personality or temperament differences and in this way to achieve an integrated, detailed, and comprehensive explanation of brain, mind, and behavior relationships.

It will no doubt be argued that this claim is unjustified arising as it does from a limited set of empirical observations. Such an argument would be ill conceived and mistaken since the observations in question derive from research that has addressed fundamental issues of cardinal theoretical significance. Once observed, the complex of systematic and hitherto unknown relationships between neurological and psychological variables leads inevitably to a radical new conception of the human psyche which extends far beyond any specific set of empirical findings, as it should, to explain much that was previously obscure and incomprehensible. Once conceived, a theory has a life of its own. It cannot be judged merely on the circumstances of its birth. It must be judged relative to other competing theories in terms of its explanatory power, in terms of its capacity to stimulate research by predicting new and unexpected relationships, and in terms of its ability to withstand empirical testing.

We have already seen how it has been possible to clarify and explain Pavlov's findings while at the same time refining and greatly extending Eysenck's theory of personality. It now seems important to compare the new theory with some other theories that purport to explain important aspects of the human psyche. Spearman's (1927) ideas are especially relevant and important because there has been no comparable theory of intelligence, even down to the present time, and because his concept of general intelligence relates in a particularly meaningful fashion to the observations and ideas described in this chapter.

In order to demonstrate the general relevance and universality of the new theory, reference will subsequently be made to the theoretical formulations of Freud and Jung and to some more recently formulated conceptions of personality.

9

The Neurological Bases of
Spearman's Factors

A popular misconception (Cattell, 1971, 1987) is that Spearman sought to account for "what the world means by intelligence" in terms of just one unitary general intelligence factor. As we shall see, this is not really correct and Cattell's subsequent proposal that intelligence involved two (and later three) different general intelligence factors is not as great a departure from Spearman's position as it first appears to be. In fact, Spearman acknowledged three general factors that influence the performance of cognitive tasks. Consideration of these factors is particularly relevant here since it is possible to demonstrate that, even in the very first systematic statistical analyses of test data, there was evidence of a relationship between intelligence and introversion-extraversion. The kind of relationship that has been revealed by the empirical observations described in the previous chapters.

In order to ascertain whether the correlations within any set of mental-ability variables could be attributed to one, or more than one factor, Spearman used a procedure which involved the calculation of "tetrad differences." The details of this procedure need not be described here except to say that it is fairly simple and that it provides an unambiguous answer to the question of interest, namely, can the correlations within a set of variables be represented by one dimension or factor, or is it the case that two or more factors are required? The method does have some limitations, but its lack of ambiguity is something that cannot be claimed by the more complex methods of statistical analysis subsequently developed.

The key to understanding Spearman's position is that he reserved the term "intelligence" to describe one particular factor. The existence of other ability factors was acknowledged, but within the conceptual framework developed by Spearman, there were good reasons why these should not be described as intelligence factors. This contrasts with the theoretically sterile approach of his successors where any factor derived from the statistical analysis of ability tests is likely to be dubbed an "intelligence" factor.

SPEARMAN'S DISTINCTION BETWEEN CONATION AND COGNITION

In discussing conation, Spearman (1927) sets out to ascertain "how much the success of anybody at a test of cognition [depends], not upon . . . cognitive ability itself, but rather upon . . . conation to cognize" (331).

In doing so, he associates his g, or general intelligence factor, with actual ability to cognize as distinct from conation or the will to cognize. Conation subsumes attitudes towards testing, sustained concentration of mental effort or attention, and purposive consistency, even though it is acknowledged that intelligence has often been defined in such terms.

This distinction between cognition and conation is one of great importance since it shows quite clearly that Spearman, despite the popular misconceptions noted above, did not think of the g factor as relating to all that then and now is commonly associated with the concept of intelligence. The point is well brought out by Spearman (1927, p. 359) when he states that "we have examined what are usually regarded as different types or kinds of general ability; in particular, 'profoundness,' 'quickness,' 'common sense,' and 'originality.' What the world means by all these, and even by plain 'intelligence' itself—especially in the case of adults—certainly does appear to mean much over and above g."

He goes on to claim that this surplus is in part reducible to an additional cognitive factor, c, with the remainder accounted for by a conative factor, w.

SPEARMAN ACKNOWLEDGES THREE FACTORS: g, c, AND w

The character of the three factors, g, c, and w, is described in Spearman's "Cardinal Conclusions." According to Spearman (1927, p. 411) "g proved to be a factor which enters into the measurements of abilities of all kinds. . . . It showed itself to be involved invariably and exclusively in all operations of eductive nature, whatever might be the class of relation or the sort of fundaments at issue."

Insofar as Spearman claims that *g* enters into abilities of all kinds, he does not accurately summarize the data that he reviews. That is to say, some cognitive abilities are associated with the *c* and *w* factors but not with *g*. Having made this point, there is less cause to disagree with Spearman's (1927, p. 413) later claim that "only one of [the factors], *g*, is of such a nature as to manifest appreciable individual differences *in the ordinary tests of intelligence*" (emphasis added). An important qualification here is the reference to "ordinary tests of intelligence" rather than to "abilities of all kinds" or to what the world means by intelligence.

Another factor, Spearman claims, "[is] only second in importance to the establishment of *g* . . . as also possessing functional unity or acting as a behaviour unit. This . . . may be called general mental inertia or lag; another convenient name for it, especially when present to excess, is perseveration. Comparative freedom from it, which with Garnett we may call *c*, has proved to be the main ground on which persons become reputed for 'quickness' or for 'originality' " (1927, p. 412).

Here it is noteworthy that *c* is the obverse of what Spearman labels perseveration. For the sake of clarity, it is also noted that Spearman's particular concept of perseveration will in due course be distinguished from the more usual conception of perseveration.

With regard to *w*, Spearman refers to "another great functional unity . . . although not in itself of a cognitive nature, yet [it] has a dominating influence upon all exercise or even estimation of cognitive ability. On trying to express it by any current name, perhaps the least satisfactory—though still seriously misleading—would be 'self-control.' It has shown itself chiefly responsible for the fact of one person's ability seeming to be more 'profound' or more inclined to 'common sense' than that of persons equally capable" (1927, p. 413).

Here it may be noted that Spearman links *w* with self-control and avoids any reference to the will or to sustained concentration of mental effort or to Webb's original definition in terms of "purposive consistency." It is sufficient to state here that while the distinction between conation and cognition is useful, in that it separates ability to perform intelligence tests from the will, inclination, or desire to do so, one finds difficulty with the notion that the motivating power of ideation is not cognitive. Moreover, even if it were conceded that persons who differ in terms of *w* are "equally capable" in the domain of intelligence tests, they would certainly not be equally capable in the domain of real intellectual achievements where purposive consistency and sustained concentration of attention are necessary if not sufficient attributes.

Since *g* relates to what is commonly measured in "ordinary" tests of intelligence, the results described in the preceding chapter indicate that this factor is reflecting a contrast between middling thalamocortical arousability and the two extremes of arousability. This conclusion is also consistent with theory insofar as middling arousability is thought to promote precisely the mode of associative learning, and attention regulation, that would facilitate eduction of relations and correlates as distinct from mere reproduction. Although less immediately obvious, it is proposed that Spearman's perseveration and the *c* and *w* factors are all manifestations of psychological differences now commonly associated with introversion-extraversion and, more fundamentally, with the neurological variables described in the preceding chapter. The grounds for this assertion will become evident from a more detailed examination of the meaning and origin of Spearman's three dimensions.

SPEARMAN'S PERSEVERATION FACTOR

In *The Abilities of Man*, one first encounters findings relating to the perseveration and *w* factors when Spearman deals with the "retentivity of dispositions." For present purposes, it is Spearman's review of studies relating to his second law of "retentivity," "lag," or "perseveration" that is of interest. According to Spearman, the inertia or perseveration that he refers to

involves nothing less than that which in the doctrine of "types"—avoiding all the obscurities, inconsistencies, and even follies that so often disfigured this doctrine— has from the earliest ages remained steadily persistent and has even become increasingly definite. By this second law we are transported back to all the romantic psychologies set forth in Chapter IX. As we there saw, the lag or inertia is essentially a generalization which combines—as supplementary to each other—two concepts that have put forward extraordinarily large claims, the "perseveration" of G. E. Muller and the "secondary function" of Heymans with his school. It constitutes the solid core of such copious and dramatic writings as those of Beneker, Gross and Jung. It also wheels into general line the prolific suggestions of Meumann and the acute observations of W. Stern. Nor has this doctrine been confined to the psychology of cognition. Everywhere the perseveration, secondary function, introversion, or however else it may be entitled, has been taken to include also the feelings, impulses, and will. The perseverator has been assumed to be stable in his emotions and steadfast in his purposes; usually, indeed, a vast system of further traits of character has been attributed to him. (1927, pp. 291–292)

What is immediately evident here is that, in Spearman's account, the historical antecedent of his perseveration factor is a typological distinction related explicitly to introversion-extraversion. Thus, from the outset, there is a basis for linking perseveration with introversion-extraversion and the underlying neurological differences described earlier.

Following his review of evidence relating to inertia or perseveration, which includes the work of Heymans and the Dutch school as well as that of Wynn Jones, Lankes, and Bernstein, Spearman concludes as follows:

in this chapter we have been examining the greatest of all faculties, if by this may be signified the one which has been the most lavish of promises for individual psychology. It is also among the greatest—only second to "intelligence"—in the sense that whilst all the other assorted faculties have proved to be baseless, this perseveration now shows itself to be at any rate a half-truth. For there does appear to exist, as a unitarily functioning factor varying in degree from one individual to another, a tendency for mental processes to have a certain lag or inertia and in this meaning to perseverate. The other and false half of the faculty, as this has hitherto been depicted, comes from confusing such a lag with steadfastness of purpose. (1927, p. 306)

Thus Spearman acknowledges the existence of a perseveration factor but claims that this is something distinct from earlier notions of perseveration as relating to "the most important character-qualities" and, it is implied, something distinct from the general character factor or *w*, because the *w* factor was originally described in terms that have the same meaning as Spearman's *steadfastness of purpose* (Webb, 1915).

Webb's findings are later reviewed by Spearman in his chapter on conation, and there we see that, in terms of Webb's actual data, *w* is a dimension which contrasts "perseverance," "kindness," "trustworthiness," and "conscientiousness" with "readiness to become angry," "eagerness for admiration," and "bodily activity in pursuit of pleasure." In terms of contemporary findings, this contrast can also be related to introversion-extraversion (see Eysenck and Eysenck, 1975, p. 9). On this basis alone, there is a link between *w* and earlier ideas concerning perseveration. The same thing is implied by the general nature of Webb's factor since it clearly has a great deal to do with differences in character formerly associated with perseveration. Finally, it is explicit that *w* derives in part from actual differences on measures of "perseverance."

What appears to be happening here is that while Spearman describes his factor as one of perseveration, his use of the term differs from the more general usage. The fact that he chooses to define perseveration in terms of the lag or inertia of mental processes does not justify the conclusion that others have confused such a lag with steadfastness of purpose. In fact, insofar as perseveration means steadfastness of purpose, the term actually relates to Webb's factor rather than to Spearman's, and it would appear from a superficial analysis that it is Webb's factor rather than Spearman's which relates to the "greatest of all faculties." It will be demonstrated, however, that Spearman and Webb are actually using the term perseveration to refer to opposite poles of the same dimension.

The Wiersma Study of Perseveration

In Spearman's (1927) chapter on the law of inertia and perseveration, a review of relevant studies begins with the work of the "Dutch School," who, it is claimed, were first to devise tests for the trait of perseveration. In a 1906 study, Wiersma devised three different tests to evaluate the degree of perseveration or persistence of the effects of sensory stimulation. Considerable differences were found between "melancholiacs" and "maniacs," with greater perseveration found for melancholiacs, and normal individuals having an intermediate degree of perseveration.

Again a link with introversion-extraversion can be suggested if melancholia is considered an extreme and pathological manifestation of the melancholic temperament, and mania is considered an extreme and pathological manifestation of the choleric temperament. The melancholic and choleric temperaments have been associated with dysthymia and hysteria, respectively, the two main categories of neurotic disorder. Indeed, Eysenck's contemporary scale of introversion-extraversion derives in the first instance from studies which contrasted groups of dysthymics and hysterics (Eysenck, 1944, 1953, p. 53). It may also be noted that these two forms of neurotic disorder have often been regarded as relating to less extreme but still pathological positions on the same continuum of introversion-extraversion or cyclothymia which, at its utmost extremes, Kretschmer (1948) linked to the more severe psychotic disorders, namely, melancholia and mania.

Thus, in this first study that Spearman considers, there is a very definite suggestion that sensory perseveration might indeed be related to Webb's general character factor or at least to its typological antecedents mentioned earlier. Moreover, the character of the tests employed were such as to appear valid measures of the kind of perseveration of neural activity that had been associated especially with the ideas of Gross and Heymans and with the concept of "secondary function." Predominance of secondary function was conceived as greater selectivity in the processing of stimulus inputs together with greater persistence of neural activity evoked by effective inputs. Ultimately this was thought to result in character and personality traits that then and now signify introversion.

It is pertinent to note that high thalamocortical arousability, as detailed in earlier chapters, entails persistence of neural activity due to low damping ratio and also entails, according to theory, a selective blocking of stimulus inputs. This is precisely what is required to account for the notion of secondary function. However, of more immediate significance, the results of the Wiersma study are not consistent with Spearman's eventual conclusion that perseveration is unrelated to character traits. This conclusion only derives from the other studies of "perseveration" that he reviews where the tests employed no longer emphasize sensory perseveration but instead were chiefly composed of tasks in which previous experience can cause errors in task performance.

This new kind of perseveration test is illustrated by a task used in a study by Wynn Jones. Subjects were required to write the letter "S" repeatedly in the usual manner and then to write the same letter as it would appear in a mirror. Perseveration was indicated if, in the second part of the test, the letter was written in the usual fashion. Conceptually and methodologically, this kind of "perseveration" has no obvious connection with the kind of perseveration assessed in the Wiersma study. From the results obtained by Wynn Jones, Spearman draws the provisional conclusion that "perseveration possesses functional unity and therefore supplies a broad group factor ... this factor is the main constituent in all that is common to the four tests although accompanied in these by a small mixture of g" (1927, pp. 297–298).

The Lankes Study of Perseveration

Spearman next considers a study by Lankes which he claimed to be distinctive in terms of "the number, variety, and systematic conception of the criteria of perseveration" (1927, p. 298). In this case, nine tests were employed, but only one of these was similar to the sensory perseveration procedures used by Wiersma. The others were broadly similar to the tasks of Wynn Jones in that performance was susceptible to errors due to interference caused by prior learning or experience. For example, "letter writing" required subjects to first write, repeatedly and rapidly, six successive letters of the alphabet. Following this, subjects were required to write the letters in reverse order. According to Spearman, an important feature of this research was that the forty-seven students who participated in the "final experiments" were among those "previously submitted by Webb to an exceptionally thorough estimate of character [see p.345]. By this means it was hoped to ascertain at last the truth or otherwise of the old belief that perseveration affects not only the cognitive processes but also the most important character-qualities" (1927, p. 301). Here again Spearman concludes that the intercorrelations of the nine tests are due to a perseveration factor and not to g.

Turning to "the other great question," Spearman describes the results as surprising. Instead of the positive correlation that might have been expected between "cognitive perseveration" and Webb's character traits, Spearman reports a negative correlation of the order of -0.40. This, then, is the primary basis for Spearman's rejection of the long-held belief that perseveration is related to the most important character traits.

Spearman explains this very interesting and theoretically important negative correlation in terms of an entirely speculative curvilinear relationship between "perseveration," as defined by the variables of Wynn Jones and Lankes, and "self-control," which is the name coined for Webb's w factor. Thereafter, there is no further mention of the negative correlation, nor does it figure in Spearman's ultimate conclusions where, entirely at odds with this finding, Spearman describes the inertia/perseveration factor as something distinct from Webb's w. This is manifestly not so. Further, since the two factors are negatively correlated, one is justified in suggesting that Spearman's inertia or perseveration is associated with the "negative" pole of Webb's w factor, whereas perseveration in the classical sense would be associated with the "positive" pole.

The Bernstein Study of Perseveration

Further insights are provided by Spearman's review of Bernstein's perseveration study. In this case, ten tests of perseveration were administered to 130 school children. All of these tests, bar one, were constructed so as to create competition between the requirements of a new task and previously learned response patterns. Five of the tests were actually taken from Lankes and Wynn Jones. Spearman (1927, p. 303) also notes that "in addition to the administration of these tests long and careful observations were made of the perseveration exhibited by the children in their ordinary school work; in particular, note was taken of the differences displayed by them in the ease with which they started any fresh lesson."

Analysis of Bernstein's data revealed that correlations between the ten perseveration tests were much lower than in the work of Wynn Jones, but the result hailed by Spearman as especially significant was that the correlations between individual tests of perseveration and the estimates of classroom perseveration were "comparatively high." Moreover, "the correlation of the pool of tests with the [classroom perseveration] rises to no less than 0.51" (1927, p. 304). In addition, Spearman (1927, p. 304) points out that "none of these values are appreciably reduced on eliminating the influence of *g*." He further states that since "values no greater than 0.51 frequently occur between the most approved tests of *g* and the estimates of intelligence (see p.188) the hope seems allowable that the measuring of perseveration has now entered upon a stage comparable with the present measurement of *g* itself" (1927, p. 304).

Referring again to the table of test correlations Spearman compares the median value of tetrad differences with the probable error of sampling and concludes that "the whole of the correlations derive from only one [perseveration] factor" (1927, p. 305).

The correlation between the perseveration tests and estimates of classroom perseveration would appear to provide strong support for the notion that the kind of perseveration measured by the tests of Wynn Jones, Lankes, and now Bernstein is, in truth, the kind of perseveration observed in everyday behavior but, according to Spearman, incorrectly associated with "the most important character traits."

It transpires, however, that Bernstein's definition of classroom perseveration is not at all akin to what is usually meant by perseveration when the term has been associated with desirable character traits such as "consistency of action resulting from volition or will" or "perseverance in the face of obstacles." To illustrate this very important point, Bernstein's description of classroom perseveration can usefully be compared with descriptions of perseveration obtained in Webb's study but never mentioned as such by Spearman.

Spearman notes that in Bernstein's study "those showing least adaptability to new work, taking an inordinate time to settle down to any task and perhaps finding themselves compelled to rush through a great deal of work in the last few minutes in order to produce a tolerable output were classed as the highest perseverators" (1927, p. 303). The picture evoked by this description is simply one of "hyperactive" or very extraverted children who cannot settle down and apply themselves to classwork. Usually such differences have been associated with lack of self-control and distractibility. There is no basis whatsoever for the claim that such behavior is related to perseveration except in a negative sense.

In referring to Webb's findings, Spearman notes that "Profoundness [of apprehension]—shows a striking affinity to all the traits involving *w*. Of particular relevance, there is a correlation of 0.75 with 'Perseverance as opposed to willful changeability' and a correlation of 0.72 with 'Perseverance in the face of obstacles' " (1927, p. 350). Profoundness was described as follows: "The subjects grasp not only the new truth or problem but its relationship to other truths and problems at the same time" or as "the grasping of an idea fully, turning it over and viewing it from every point of view" or "having grasped a point [those rated highly for this trait] see its bearing on the subject and associate it readily with other information on the same subject" (1927, p. 349).

Clearly, there are key elements in the descriptions of "perseverators" provided by Bernstein and those from Webb's study that are diametrically opposed. In one case, perseverators are described as *those showing least adaptability to new work*. In the other, perseverators are *the subjects who grasp not only the new truth or problem, but its relationship to other truths and problems at the same time*.

Two Meanings of Perseveration Subsumed by Introversion-Extraversion

When consideration is given to perseveration, as this relates to the "cognitive tests" of Wynn Jones, Lankes, and Bernstein, in contrast to the perseveration associated with Webb's "character qualities," it is again clear that the term has two quite different and opposite meanings. In the case of cognitive tests such as "Cancellation" and "Letter Writing," perseveration would have to be defined as a persistence of automatic unconscious motor habits which results in failure to achieve some conscious goal or objective. In the case of "character qualities," perseveration would have to be defined as an ability to continue working toward some conscious goal in spite of obstacles or difficulties. The first definition indicates that conscious ideation, the "will," or voluntary control fails to suppress automatic unconscious motor habits that are no longer appropriate. The second indicates a triumph of will and conscious voluntary control in the regulation of behavior. It is not surprising then that, as noted above, Spearman reports a substantial negative correlation between putative cognitive tests of perseveration and the character qualities evaluated in Webb's study.

To sum up, it seems clear that in progressing from the "sensory" perseveration tests of Wiersma and Heymans to the perseveration of "automatic response habits" or of analogous phenomena that are characteristic of the tests employed by Wynn Jones, Lankes, and Bernstein, the term perseveration comes to have an exactly opposite significance vis-à-vis the more general conception of perseveration which relates to character traits. The perseveration of behavior in the service of conscious ideation is replaced by the perseveration of unconscious automatic response habits which interfere with the former. This is borne out by the kind of classroom behaviors found to be positively correlated with Bernstein's perseveration measures and especially so by the negative correlation between Lankes's perseveration measures and Webb's *w* factor. Thus, the facts do not support Spearman's conclusion that his inertia or perseveration factor is something distinct from Webb's *w*. In fact, the previously mentioned negative correlation suggests a more parsimonious explanation for the findings reviewed by Spearman. In particular, that there is only one factor and not two, a factor contrasting greater perseveration of conscious ideation and possibly prolonged sensory aftereffects, at one pole, with greater perseveration of automatic unconscious response habits and related phenomena at the other.

In addition, the historical antecedents of this factor, as well as contemporary descriptions of personality based on sustained and systematic research, both suggest an alignment with the introversion-extraversion dimension, and more specifically with the melancholic to choleric continuum that has been shown here to have a rectilinear relationship with differences in overall thalamocortical arousability. More importantly, in the theory of brain function elaborated in preceding chapters, it has been explicitly stated that high thalamocortical arousability results in the relative dominance of thalamocortical processes over brain-stem processes. This means greater influence of the conscious processes controlling voluntary behavior over unconscious processes that control involuntary automatic responses. For individuals with lower thalamocortical arousability, conscious voluntary control of behavior is reduced or weakened and, with a correspondingly reduced inhibition of brain-stem activity, a greater part of behavior is determined by unconscious automatic processes. As detailed in earlier chapters, this neurological mechanism accounts for some of the most characteristic differences between melancholic and choleric individuals, but it is also precisely the kind of mechanism that is required to explain the bipolar dimension suggested by the findings reviewed by Spearman and contrasting the two different kinds of perseveration.

From the foregoing account, it is clear that the three factors acknowledged by Spearman reduce to two. One of these is general intelligence, or g, and this derives from a contrast between middling thalamocortical arousability on the one hand, and high or low arousability on the other. In terms of temperament, the same contrast distinguishes sanguine and phlegmatic individuals from melancholics and cholerics.

The second bipolar factor is orthogonal to g and derives from a contrast between high and low thalamocortical arousability. Although thalamocortical arousability can no longer be considered the only or most fundamental determinant of introversion-extraversion differences, it is nevertheless closely aligned with this dimension of personality and can account for Webb's w factor and its obverse, Spearman's perseveration.

In terms of thalamocortical arousability, the four temperaments can be ordered from melancholic through phlegmatic and sanguine to choleric. As we have seen, melancholics are highest in terms of thalamocortical arousability. Phlegmatics, the other introverted type are, on average, also high on arousability but less so than melancholics. Sanguine individuals occupy the middle range of arousability with some overlapping of sanguine and phlegmatic types. Finally, cholerics are lowest in terms of arousability. It is this continuum of temperament variation ranging from melancholic to choleric that corresponds to Webb's w and, inversely, to Spearman's perseveration factor.

WEBB'S w FACTOR

Webb's Study and the Discovery of w

It is appropriate now to consider in greater detail Spearman's treatment of Webb's study, which is considered at length in his chapter on conation. In the opening statement concerning character and conation, Spearman acknowledges that his "source of information will be mainly the work of Webb, since this appears to stand up to the present time without rival" (1927, p. 345). This comment is equally applicable today, and as Spearman notes "the leading characteristic of the research was the extreme care given to, and exceptionally favorable opportunities for, very diversified and systematic mental estimates . . . among the mental traits estimated were four that appeared to represent 'intelligence' of different kinds; they were respectively Profoundness of Apprehension, Quickness of Apprehension, Common Sense and Originality of Ideas" (1927, pp. 345–346).

These estimates, together with a measure of g and records of scholastic examinations, produced the correlations shown here in Table 9.1.

Table 9.1
Correlation Matrix for Webb's Six Different Measures of Intelligence

	g	E	P	Q	CS	O
1. Test of g	-	0.67	0.56	0.53	0.29	0.47
2. Examinations	0.67	-	0.65	0.25	0.52	0.57
3. Estimated profoundness	0.56	0.65	-	0.96	1.00	0.88
4. Estimated quickness	0.53	0.25	0.96	-	0.81	1.00
5. Estimated common sense	0.29	0.52	1.00	0.81	-	0.81
6. Estimated originality	0.47	0.57	0.88	1.00	0.81	-

Spearman points out that "although all six correlated values purport to be measurements of some or other aspect of intelligence, there is not even a rough approximation to satisfying the criterion of tetrad differences" (1927, p. 346). This, of course, signifies that the intercorrelations cannot be accounted for by just one factor.

The nature of a factor additional to g was first suggested by Webb's observation that despite a high correlation between "profoundness of apprehension" and "quickness of apprehension," the correlations between these two variables and measures of differences in character were sometimes very different. In particular, "profoundness" but not "quickness" was very highly correlated with:

1. Perseverance as opposed to willful changeability.
2. Perseverance in the face of obstacles.
3. Kindness on principle.
4. Trustworthiness.
5. Conscientiousness.

In contrast, "quickness" but not "profoundness" had relatively high correlations with:

6. Readiness to become angry.

7. Eagerness for admiration.

8. Bodily activity in pursuit of pleasure (games, etc.).

Following this observation, Webb then examined the intercorrelations of these eight traits. After correction for attenuation, and after eliminating the influence of g, the correlations were as shown here in Table 9.2.

Further analysis of these correlations led Webb to conclude that, in Spearman's words, "the whole correlation in the table derives from one and the same factor" (1927, p. 348). Similar results were obtained in a second sample and Spearman (1927) describes Webb's claim that the new general factor contrasted "moral qualities and the deeper social virtues" at one pole, with "instability of emotions" and the "lighter side of sociality" at the other. He further stated that the second factor was closely related to "persistence of motives." This, he claimed, could be understood to mean "consistency of action resulting from volition or will" (p.348). Accordingly, Webb used

Table 9.2

Correlation Matrix for Eight Different Character Traits Identified in Text

	1	2	3	4	5	6	7	8
1	-	0.92	0.58	0.74	0.68	-0.45	-0.55	-0.08
2	0.92	-	0.46	0.52	0.50	-0.29	-0.45	0.07
3	0.58	0.46	-	1.00	0.95	-0.85	-0.61	0.11
4	0.74	0.52	1.00	-	1.00	-0.78	-0.78	0.13
5	0.68	0.50	0.95	1.00	-	-0.78	-0.74	-0.26
6	-0.45	-0.29	-0.85	-0.78	-0.78	-	0.93	0.36
7	-0.55	-0.45	-0.61	-0.78	-0.74	0.93	-	0.37
8	-0.08	0.07	0.11	-0.13	-0.26	0.36	0.37	-

The correlations have been corrected for attenuation, and the influence of g has been eliminated.

the symbol *w* to denote the new factor and his own emphasis on volition or will.

The Relation of *w* to the Melancholic versus Choleric Continuum

It is very clear from Webb's findings that the *w* factor has a broader compass than volition or will. Further, consideration of the individual traits associated with the factor leaves little room to doubt that Webb has actually identified a dimension of individual differences which relates back to what Spearman described as the "doctrine of types" and to the antecedents of his perseveration factor. It will be recalled that Spearman stated: "Everywhere, the perseveration, secondary function, introversion, or however else it may be entitled has been taken to include also the feelings, impulses and will. The perseverator has been assumed to be stable in his emotions and steadfast in his purposes; usually, indeed, a vast system of further traits of character has been attributed to him" (1927, p. 292).

On comparing this statement with the individual traits that define Webb's *w* factor, it seems incredible, as noted earlier, that Spearman failed to acknowledge explicitly the great significance of Webb's findings vis-à-vis these earlier ideas concerning perseveration. All the more so when the relationship of his own perseveration factor to these earlier concepts is actually assessed by calculating its correlation with Webb's *w*.

As indicated earlier, the similarity between Webb's factor and earlier ideas concerning perseveration and character differences suggests that *w* relates to introversion-extraversion, or more specifically to the melancholic versus choleric continuum. It was also suggested that such a relationship or identity is indicated when the individual traits associated with *w* are compared with contemporary descriptions of introverts and extraverts derived from the results of long-sustained and systematic research. The Eysencks (Eysenck and Eysenck, 1975, p. 9) include the following traits in their description of introverts: being reliable and placing great value on ethical standards. The corresponding traits defining Webb's factor are: perseverance, trustworthiness, and conscientiousness. In like manner, the Eysencks go on to describe the extravert as: tending to be aggressive and short-tempered, preferring to keep moving and doing things, and craving excitement. We may add that extraverts like to "show off," and in this case the corresponding traits from Webb are: readiness to become angry, eagerness for admiration, and bodily activity in pursuit of pleasure (games, etc.).

This additional detail strengthens the argument that Spearman's perseveration (inversely) and Webb's *w* factor both relate to differences in overall thalamocortical arousability. It follows that the whole matrix of correlations between Webb's measures of intelligence and character traits can be understood in terms of thalamocortical arousability.

Spearman's Three-Factor Interpretation of Webb's Findings

Spearman's own evaluation of Webb's findings led him to propose a less parsimonious account involving three factors instead of two. Spearman starts from consideration of the correlations reproduced in Table 9.3.

In this table, correlations are shown for the six "intelligence" variables with Webb's complete set of "character" variables. He notes that there are three pairs of highly correlated intelligence variables so that, in effect, the six original variables relate to only three main aspects of intelligence. The first pair relates to *g*, and this requires no further comment. The other two pairs are particularly interesting and revealing.

"Profoundness" and "common sense" make up the second pair of highly correlated variables, and, as one would anticipate, there is very close agreement between the two as regards their respective correlations with each of the character traits. This is evident from inspection of columns 1 and 2 in the table, and, as Spearman also observes, both intelligence variables show a striking affinity to all the traits involving *w*. In particular, he points out that both abilities have high positive correlations with "kindness on principle," "trustworthiness," "conscientiousness," as well as with the cognate "interest in religion," "farsightedness," "puremindedness," and "love of intimate circles." Both also have markedly negative correlations with "readiness to become angry," "oscillation of mood," "eagerness for admiration," and "offensive self-esteem."

From inspection of the table, one must agree with Spearman excepting that there is the quite remarkable omission of "perseverance versus changeability" and "perseverance versus obstacles." Both of these traits were among those originally used to define Webb's *w* factor. The positive correlations with "profoundness" and "common sense" are among the highest listed in the table and appreciably higher than the correlations with the other four measures of intelligence. There is no obvious reason for this puzzling omission, but it did make it easier for Spearman to argue that his "perseveration" was something distinct from Webb's *w*. Spearman concludes that the correlations of "profoundness" and "common sense" with

Table 9.3
Correlation of the Six Cognitive Traits with Webb's Other Traits

		Pro-found-ness	Com-mon-sense	Quick-ness	Origi-nality	Exams	Test of *g*
		1	2	3	4	5	6
	Selected to Prove W						
1.	Perseverance vs. change	0.75	0.71	0.40	0.48	0.39	0.34
2.	Perseverance vs. obstacles	0.72	0.77	0.59	0.69	0.41	0.28
3.	Kindness on principle	0.69	0.79	0.46	0.47	0.17	0.23
4.	Trustworthiness	0.66	0.57	0.40	0.46	0.31	0.28
5.	Conscientiousness	0.66	0.64	0.24	0.43	0.19	0.22
6.	Readiness to become angry	-0.39	-0.53	-0.01	-0.09	0.07	0.00
7.	Eagerness for admiration	-0.29	-0.37	0.19	-0.07	0.17	0.10
8.	Bod. activities for pleasure	0.02	-0.04	-0.16	0.17	-0.16	-0.19
9.	Cheerfulness	0.26	0.34	0.59	0.58	0.11	0.34
	Emotions						
10.	Oscillation of mood	-0.48	-0.51	-0.38	-0.36	-0.30	-0.39
11.	Occasional great depression	-0.17	-0.40	-0.43	-0.48	-0.12	-0.31
12.	Quick recovery from anger	0.24	0.48	0.21	0.18	0.07	0.09
13.	Occasional great anger	-0.18	-0.30	0.06	0.14	0.06	-0.01
14.	Aesthetic feeling	0.71	0.76	0.55	0.64	0.46	0.46
15.	Sense of humor	0.49	0.45	0.85	0.79	0.18	-0.17
	Self-Regard						
16.	Desire to excel	0.63	0.61	0.42	0.54	0.62	0.39
17.	Desire to impose will on others	-0.13	-0.25	0.19	-0.05	0.08	0.13
18.	Belief in own powers	0.27	0.16	0.38	0.36	0.46	0.35
19.	Esteem of self	-0.05	-0.20	0.17	0.27	0.25	0.11
20.	Offensive self-esteem	-0.28	-0.49	0.10	0.13	0.07	0.22
	Social Tendencies						
21.	Love of large gatherings	-0.16	-0.12	0.42	0.44	-0.08	0.30
22.	Love of intimate circles	0.64	0.55	0.22	0.31	0.33	0.35
23.	Kindness on impulse	0.19	0.37	0.21	0.30	-0.07	-0.19
24.	Corporate spirit	0.32	0.38	0.40	0.45	0.21	0.03
25.	Interest in religion	0.54	0.52	0.03	0.18	0.22	0.28
26.	Suggestibility	-0.09	0.10	-0.22	-0.30	-0.04	0.02
27.	Desire to be liked	0.13	0.02	0.38	0.20	0.07	0.07
28.	Wideness of influence	0.77	0.69	0.66	0.70	0.21	0.11
29.	Intensity of influence	0.88	0.74	0.87	0.86	0.35	0.39
30.	Tact	0.32	0.35	0.40	0.45	0.00	-0.02
	Activity						
31.	Work on study	0.74	0.67	0.30	0.40	0.78	0.60
32.	Work on pleasure	0.01	0.02	0.27	0.11	-0.16	-0.15
33.	Bod. activities in business	0.34	0.21	0.34	0.54	0.19	0.13
34.	Far-sightedness	0.75	0.67	0.27	0.36	0.59	0.45
35.	Pure-mindedness	0.47	0.54	0.11	0.15	0.24	0.15
36.	Rapid mental work	0.84	0.70	0.96	0.94	0.81	0.54
37.	Bodily physique	0.01	0.04	0.15	0.17	0.09	-0.07
	General						
38.	Character (rated by prefects)	0.62	0.53	0.15	0.26	0.60	0.37
39.	Character (rated by staff)	0.77	0.88	0.50	0.55	0.43	0.36
40.	Strength of will	0.75	0.95	0.61	0.69	0.67	0.29
41.	Excitability	-0.29	-0.47	0.23	-0.09	-0.10	0.23

the other (character) traits can be explained in terms of a combination of g and w.

However, from the perspective of contemporary knowledge, not to mention earlier ideas and concepts, there can be little doubt that the correlations are due to a combination of g with arousal-related differences on the introversion-extraversion dimension. The positive correlates of "profoundness" and "common sense" would relate to high g and introversion. The negative correlates would relate to low g and extraversion. In effect, there is a contrast here between the phlegmatic and choleric temperaments.

Spearman moves on to consider the third pair of variables, "quickness of apprehension" and "originality of ideas," that can be associated with a major aspect of intelligence. Here again he notes that the intelligence measures are very highly correlated and that each yields a similar pattern of correlations with all the other (character) traits.

Spearman proceeds to consider the characteristics of this single "quickness-originality" trait. Perhaps the most important, he claims, is that although not correlating with w qualities as highly as did the previous pair, the correlations are still substantial. Here again, then, w and g are largely involved.

However, it can be observed that here Spearman's conclusion is quite at odds with the data presented in table 9.3. In fact, the correlations of "quickness" and "originality" with the w traits are all very substantially lower than those obtained for "profoundness" and "commonsense." Moreover, they are similar in magnitude to the correlations found between g and the w character traits. This means that the correlations between "quickness-originality" and the w character traits can be accounted for almost entirely in terms of g.

The nature of the "quickness-originality" continuum, as involving something additional to g, is only revealed by consideration of correlations with the character traits not already associated with Webb's w factor. Spearman writes that

as regards several other traits . . . Quickness and Originality show a marked deviation from the former pair. Most conspicuous in this respect is Humour with which they correlate to a surprising degree (+.85 and +.79). Very notable also are their high correlations with Cheerfulness, Love of Large Gatherings, Tact and above all the Capacity for Rapid Mental Work (+.96 and +.94). Interesting further are their exceptionally low correlations with Interest in Religion and with Pure-Mindedness. All these cases indicate that the Quickness and Originality contain, over and above the w and g some very important further ingredient. (1927, p. 353)

Again from the perspective of contemporary knowledge there can be little doubt that the correlations are here also due to a combination of *g* and introversion-extraversion.

In this case, however, it is extraversion that is associated with high *g* rather than introversion. This is indicated especially by the positive correlations with "love of large gatherings," "humor," and "cheerfulness" but also by the very low correlations with "pure mindedness" and "interest in religion." If again we take the correlations between *g* and the character traits as a reference point or baseline, it is clear that the latter correlations with "quickness and originality" would very likely be negative if the influence of *g* was partialled out.

The link between "quickness-originality" and extraversion is further substantiated if we consider some additional correlates of this continuum that, again quite inexplicably, Spearman fails to mention. As compared with the other two pairs of intelligence measures, "quickness-originality" has appreciably higher correlations with "corporate spirit," "desire to be liked," and "work on pleasure." There are appreciably lower or negative correlations with "desire to excel," "work on study," "farsightedness," "excellence of character (as noted by prefects)," "occasional great depression," and "suggestibility." In the main, these correlations also point quite definitely to the introversion-extraversion dimension and to an alignment of high *g* with extraversion. In this case, there is effectively a contrast between the sanguine and melancholic temperaments.

The general conclusion one arrives at is that Spearman's observations concerning Webb's findings can all be accounted for in terms of *g* and introversion-extraversion when account is taken of the relationship between these variables and thalamocortical arousability.

The General Significance of Webb's Findings

It is especially noteworthy that, in proposing two factors to account for Webb's correlations, one agrees with Webb's own conclusions. Of all the work reviewed by Spearman, Webb's study stands out as a remarkable achievement and not least because it reveals the limitations of any simple unidimensional measure of *g* or general intelligence. Webb's results demonstrate in a very clear way that any meaningful or useful psychological assessment, even when limited to intellectual potential, must take account of temperament or personality differences.

As already noted, one has only to survey Webb's table of correlations to appreciate the great variety of human attributes that can be accounted for when *g* and temperament differences are considered in combination. In contrast, one is struck by the relative narrowness and the very restricted nature of contemporary systems of personality description (Cattell, 1995; Goldberg, 1993). Not only is intelligence usually treated as something distinct from other dimensions of personality, but these other dimensions are themselves often conceived in narrow and restricted terms that greatly understate the enormity of their psychological significance. For example, introversion-extraversion is often associated with just two traits, impulsivity and sociability. Yet, we can see from Webb's study that this dimension in combination with *g* relates to attributes such as "will to achieve," "desire for excellence," "farsightedness," "wideness and intensity of social influence," "work habits," and, not least important, all those traits such as "kindness," "trustworthiness," "religious interest," and "pure mindedness" that relate to the manner in which people conduct their affairs, for good or ill.

One can see also that Webb's results, viewed from the perspective of arousability theory, have a bearing on profound philosophical questions concerning the nature and genesis of morality. It is quite startling to contemplate that moral ideation and behavior is influenced by differences in thalamocortical arousability, but this, of course, is perfectly consistent with the immediate psychological consequences of alcohol ingestion or the ingestion of other drugs known to alter thalamocortical activity levels. It is also consistent with the concept of "cerebral" emotions introduced earlier and to which we shall return in due course.

Spearman's analysis of Webb's findings in terms of three correlated factors is especially valuable in that it provides a further demonstration of the validity of the relationship between temperament and intelligence differences indicated by Figures 6.4 and 6.5. Equally important, the tables of correlations obtained from Webb's very comprehensive study illustrate most effectively the great range of human traits and attributes that can be expected to vary as a function of differences in thalamocortical arousability.

To his credit, Spearman was not just concerned with factors of intelligence generated by statistical analysis, and in the next chapter we move on to consider his very original and comprehensive theory of intelligence. Although seldom referred to by contemporary researchers, the intellectual power of Spearman's formulation has never been equaled, and it contains many valuable and interesting insights gleaned from his extensive program of systematic research.

10

A Reappraisal of Spearman's Intelligence Theory

Spearman was not just concerned with intelligence factors suggested by statistical analysis of test data—the narrow preoccupation of many successors. Over a long period, different lines of investigation were systematically opened up in accordance with a preconceived and unitary plan. The objective was nothing less than the formulation of general laws describing all aspects of cognition, especially learning, memory, attention, and cognition but referring also to the effects of fatigue and heredity as well as to sex and age differences. Most importantly, Spearman sought to understand how his laws of cognition could be applied to the study and understanding of individual differences in ability. The discovery of g, the formulation of his noegenetic laws of eduction, and his account of g in terms of these laws are unparalleled achievements in the study of cognition and human ability, not least because these particular ideas and related findings were set in a broader and more comprehensive conceptual and empirical framework. We have seen how Spearman's factors can be explained in terms of thalamocortical arousability, but it is pertinent also to consider his broader conception of intelligence and cognition. It transpires that there are important areas of agreement where Spearman's ideas and concepts enrich and extend those discussed in earlier chapters.

THE NOEGENETIC LAWS AND GENERAL INTELLIGENCE

The significance of Spearman's noegenetic laws seems lost to many who currently seek to understand cognition and intelligence in terms of information processing models. The approach that appears to characterize this work is first to specify some particular cognitive task and then to ask how this task could be performed by a series of logical operations, as in a digital computer.

The outcome is that we may learn more about the manner in which computers can be programmed to perform certain tasks, and perhaps something about their limitations, but relatively little about actual human cognition. In fact, one might argue that any achievements are more than offset by the consequences of propagating misinformation concerning actual human cognition. That is to say, until very recently most cognitive models were constructed entirely without reference to what is known about brain function or to any psychological considerations other than the amount of time required to execute "components" of a particular task, or a restricted and limited set of specific tasks (Sternberg, 1977). For this reason, many of the proposed models are, from the outset, simply not valid in neurological or even psychological terms. It is in the nature of attempts to model the performance of particular tasks by reference to digital computers or "information theory" that human cognition should be largely conceived in terms of the performance of a series of logical operations and in terms of "programming" the brain to employ successful "problem-solving" strategies (Hunt, 1980). This, of course, does relate in part to what we mean by cognition. In our thinking, we do perform logical operations and we do learn to employ successful strategies. The problem is that this aspect of cognition has a great deal to do with what Spearman termed "reproduction." And, as Spearman long ago discovered, *the power of human cognition, the ability to know and to understand and to have insight, and the principal factor involved in the performance of intelligence tests is eduction not reproduction.*

Spearman's conclusions are set out in his three laws of noegenetics. He states that "these three ultimate qualitative laws (and their corresponding processes) . . . prescribe how all new cognition (i.e., all cognition that is not merely reproductive) is ever possible" (1927, p. 164).

The first law states that "a person has more or less power to observe what goes on in his own mind" (1927, p. 164).

The second law concerns the eduction of relations. It states that "when a person has in mind any two or more ideas (using this word to embrace any items of mental content, whether perceived or thought of), he has more or less power to bring to mind any relations that essentially hold between them" (1927, p. 165).

The third law concerns the eduction of correlates. "This enounces that when a person has in mind any idea together with a relation, he has more or less power to bring to mind the correlative idea (that is, an analogy)" (1927, p. 166).

It is noted that computers are capable of reproduction, but only in a very restricted and trivial sense can they educe relations and correlates. Spearman recognized the important difference between eduction and reproduction but he could not offer any explanation. It seems obvious that eduction must depend on associative learning, but the same would hold for reproduction. The nature of the difference was suggested in Chapter 8, where it was proposed that both high and low thalamocortical arousability would result in rapid but indiscriminate learning of associations, albeit within two distinct categories, and that this favors reproduction. In contrast, an intermediate degree of arousability was considered optimal for a selective learning of associations which reflects the frequency of occurrence of coincident events and hence, in a natural environment, relates to the probability that such events are truly related as distinct from simply coincident due to mere chance. In effect, middling arousability is optimal for "inferential" learning. This, together with the optimal flexibility in the regulation of attention that has been associated with middling arousability, would ensure superior performance in circumstances requiring the eduction of relations and correlates. In part, this would be due to concurrent processing, but the prior and progressive elaboration of a superior world model would be much more important. That is to say, in any specific circumstances, the power to educe relations and correlates must depend greatly on the quality of accumulated knowledge that is referenced.

Spearman's great achievement was not just to recognize the role of eduction in cognition, and its significance vis-à-vis intellectual differences, but also to carry out a systematic evaluation of different kinds of cognitive operations and intelligence measures which demonstrated conclusively the unique and wide-ranging significance of eduction and led him to propose the closest association, even an identity, between the g factor, describing all that is common in these tests, and differences in eductive ability.

RETENTIVITY AND GENERAL INTELLIGENCE

Also consistent with arousability theory is Spearman's failure to find any simple relationship between g and "retentivity." He points out that among all the copious discussion and even experimentation about "memory," "reproduction" and "association," there has been unexpectedly small success at penetrating down to and grasping distinctly the ultimate principle of pure retentivity. . . . Perhaps indeed this principle scarcely admitted of being adequately grasped before the development of the other concept which has so much occupied us, that of eduction. To understand the respective natures of eduction and reproduction—in their trenchant contrast, in their ubiquitous co-operation, and in their genetic inter-linkage—to do this would appear to be for the psychology of individual differences and even for that of cognition in general, the very beginning of wisdom. (1927, pp. 270–271)

The relevant law of "retentivity" or "dispositions" is formulated thus: "cognitive events by occurring establish dispositions which facilitate their recurrence" (1927, p. 271). Spearman goes on to note: "this includes as a special case of particular importance the law of association, which is here taken to mean that cognitive events accompanying each other establish dispositions to do so thereafter" (p. 271). Thus his law of retentivity is explicitly concerned with the formation of associative connections and, as is clear from the text, with reproduction.

The question is posed: "Does a person's g (or 'intelligence') consist in his aptitude to acquire dispositions?" (p. 272). Spearman answers thus:

[D]octrines that seem to imply [this theorem] have enjoyed, and still enjoy, a very wide currency indeed. Here may be included, for instance, all those writings which straightly assert that intelligence consists in "the capacity to learn"; for "learning"—when the term is thus used without any saving qualifications—cannot but largely consist in the forming of dispositions. . . . Another instance is afforded by those statements which, adopting a physiological terminology, depict intelligence as the property of the brain to preserve "traces" or "engrams" of its experience; for these must, in great measure at least, be the physical rendering of what have psychologically been called dispositions. . . . A further instance can seemingly be derived from the doctrine that tests of intelligence measure a person's ability to establish mental "bonds"; for these, as often interpreted at any rate, would appear to mean little more than associative connections. And here, finally, must be placed those authors who maintain that the higher powers of intelligence fail to be called into play by the ordinary tests; these latter, they say, are limited to unfamiliar operations on unfamiliar material in brief periods of time; to reach the higher powers, they urge us to go rather to the achievements of long periods with material that has become thoroughly familiar. For all such prolonged operations are really made up of brief ones, and all the said familiarity must needs derive from the establishment of dispositions. (1927, p. 272)

Following a review of relevant studies, Spearman concludes "that the *g* manifested in eduction has nothing in common with the retentivity manifested in acquiring dispositions" (1927, p. 290).

A second question that concerns Spearman is whether there exists a unitary faculty of retentivity or memory. His answer to this second question is that the

preceding inquiry about group factors ... places the power of retaining in a curious contrast with that of educing. The case of retention is much more what might have been expected a priori; for in general, the degree of functional unity corresponds fairly well with the degree of apparent likeness. When two kinds of memory resemble each other only in the bare fact of both involving retentivity, the correlation arising from this cause is little if at all above zero. In proportion as the likeness between them is augmented by resemblance of material—for instance of both being sensory, or by both being verbal—the correlation becomes more and more marked. With eduction on the other hand, all this is quite otherwise. The correlation arising from it can be very large even between operations that are extremely unlike. . . . And the correlations, large or small, which exist between extremely unlike operations are no whit increased by virtue of introducing resemblance between them—until this resemblance becomes very close indeed. (1927, pp. 289–290)

Spearman regards these findings as a further striking corroboration of the thesis that the *g* manifest in eduction has nothing in common with retentivity or reproduction, and his conclusions concerning the absence of any general retentivity factor have not been challenged by subsequent research.

Arousability theory, as noted earlier, specifies and explains a distinction between eduction and reproduction in terms of the psychological ramifications of differences in arousability. Both high and low thalamocortical arousability facilitate the "reproductive" learning of particular kinds of associations.

High arousability should facilitate the association of discrete serial inputs, such as language in the auditory modality, whereas low arousability should facilitate the association of multimodality parallel inputs. Thus one would expect two corresponding retentivity factors that are negatively correlated or, in effect, a bipolar factor that represents one particular aspect of the broader contrast between introverts and extraverts or, more specifically, between melancholic and choleric individuals. At the present time, these differences can best be illustrated by reference to the superior "verbal" ability of individuals with high introversion scores in contrast to the superior "spatial" ability of those with high extraversion scores (Robinson, 1985, 1986c).

In addition to the foregoing, there is the difference in learning negative and positive associations that has been attributed to the relative predominance of thalamocortical excitation or inhibition in melancholic and sanguine individuals, respectively (Robinson and desRosiers, in preparation). Here also one would expect two negatively correlated factors or one bipolar factor aligned with the melancholic to sanguine continuum. These predictions from arousability theory rule out the possibility of any unitary or general retentivity factor, and they are consistent with Spearman's observation that in "retentivity" the unity of factors seems to depend mainly on the similarity of the tests involved.

ATTENTION AND MENTAL ENERGY AND GENERAL INTELLIGENCE

Theories of Attention and g

Spearman acknowledges the importance of the theory that g can be ascribed to "inequalities in the power of attention." He refers to "remarkable experimental support" for this view that is provided by Burt. Burt claimed that g was especially manifest in tests of sustained attention and concentration. Studies by Woodrow and Garnett are also mentioned as providing support for this conception.

Spearman points out that there are difficulties with such a theory insofar as a study by Koch and Habrich demonstrated that higher intelligence was associated with better performance irrespective of differences in the degree of attention, concentration, or expressly directed effort involved. Here we can agree with Spearman that any theory seeking to account for g only in terms of the "capacity to concentrate attention" is inadequate.

Arousability theory proposes that middling arousability is responsible for high general intelligence, and explains why this is optimal for the control and regulation of attention. However, middling arousability is also optimal for basic information transmission and for learning, so that higher intelligence, as demonstrated by Koch and Habrich, is not just a consequence of better concentration of attention. Thus, one would expect the closest relationship between g and the capacity to concentrate attention, as Burt demonstrated, but an equally strong relationship would be expected in the case of other tasks that are not critically dependent on the concentration of attention. In short, arousability theory can account for Burt's claim while also explaining the findings of Koch and Habrich.

Spearman goes on to comment on the equivocality of the term "attention" with many different definitions. There is only one, he claims, that, given the results of Koch and Habrich, can be reconciled with the view that *g* measures attention. This is due to Maher and is favored by Spearman because attention is explained in terms of the application of mental energy.

Attention and Mental Energy

This linking of attention and mental energy had great theoretical appeal for Spearman. His own conception of mental energy and how this might relate to attention and *g* was dominated by the analogy of physical energy as something that can be "distributed" or "concentrated" and as something that empowers all kinds of diverse physical systems. In like fashion, Spearman suggested, some kind of mental energy would have the capacity to empower all kinds of diverse cognitive processes. Differences in the amount of this energy would then account for the *g* factor.

Spearman's conception of attention is indicated by his law of span, which was expressed in this way: "Every mind tends to keep its total simultaneous output constant in quantity, however varying in quality" (1927, p. 259). The same idea is further elaborated when he later suggests that, "the magnitude of . . .[mental] output—like that of physical energy—has two dimensions, intensive and extensive; the clearness and speed of an operation may either attain to a high grade, or else cover a wide field; the 'attention' may be either concentrated or else diffused" (1927, p. 260).

Here we see that attention is related to the distribution of mental energy, whereas *g* is thought to reflect differences in the total quantity of available energy. On this view, it does not matter whether attention is concentrated or diffused—*g* will be greater if the total amount of energy is greater and irrespective of the manner in which this energy or attention is distributed. According to Spearman,

mental activity, just like the physical, consists in ever varying manifestations of one and the same underlying thing, to which may be given the name of energy. No such energy, however, can possibly work in a vacuum, but only in some or other "engine." . . . With respect to the engines a suggestion is supplied at once; for the different kinds of mental output would naturally be subserved (mainly, at any rate) by different neural systems. . . . These latter, then, are suggested as being the engines. With respect to the energy, the available information is less definite. (1927, p. 133)

McQueen's Study of Intelligence and Attention

Spearman draws most empirical support for his ideas concerning the distribution of attention from a study by McQueen. From the results of this study he concludes that "both the intensity and extensity of cognitive operations depend on g" (1927, p. 269). That is to say, a greater amount of mental energy can be deployed either more intensively or more extensively than a lesser amount.

As Spearman himself admits, there are different definitions of attention, and this is always likely to cause confusion. In the McQueen study, performance thought to involve concentration of attention is assessed from the performance of pairs of tasks, such as "tapping" and "adding," where each of the tasks is performed separately. Performance thought to involve diffusion of attention is assessed when the same two tasks must be carried out at the same time. This kind of task is commonly thought to divide attention, and presumably this is what Spearman was thinking of when he regarded such tasks as measures of an ability to diffuse attention.

However, while Spearman's conception of mental energy as analogous to physical energy is of some theoretical interest, it leads him in this case to the rather peculiar notion that performance on a "divided attention" task requires less, rather than more, concentration of attention. It is actually difficult to imagine anyone suggesting that the single tasks described above would require greater concentration of attention than the dual tasks, but clearly claims and counterclaims could be made when "concentration of attention" has not been adequately defined. Here again it is possible to demonstrate the general relevance and power of arousability theory.

Within the context of arousability theory, it is possible to define two different ways in which attention can be concentrated. One of these relates to the selective perception of concurrent external events, greater "depth of processing," and the capacity to sustain this concentration of attention over long periods in the service of particular ideas or plans. This kind of concentrated attention can be attributed to high thalamocortical arousability and predominance of the cerebrum over brain-stem processes. There is an obvious correspondence with Burt's reference to "sustained effort of maximal concentration" and to "voluntary attention." Insofar as this kind of concentration of attention is associated with superior intelligence and intellectual achievement, one would expect high arousability and a phlegmatic temperament rather than *highest* arousability and a melancholic temperament. This, of course, relates back to perseveration and to Webb's consistency of action resulting from volition or will.

The other way in which concentration of attention can be defined relates to contemporary thinking concerning the capacity of working memory where individuals have more or less ability to concentrate attention on, or keep in mind, a particular set of ideas that are no longer anchored to concurrent external events. In effect, the focus of attention is "internal" rather than "external" as in the previous case.

It is clear from experimental studies and from introspection that there is a limit to the number of discrete ideas that can be kept in mind, as in the WAIS Digit Span task. The same limit restricts performance of tasks such as mental arithmetic where the ideas to be kept in mind include not only some quantitative information but also the logical operations that must be applied to this data as well as the results that derive from such application.

Arousability theory suggests that the major factor determining individual differences in the performance of such tasks is not actually differences in the number of discrete ideas on which attention can be focused. Indeed, it may be the case that attention can only be fully focused on one idea at a time with strategies such as serial reactivation or rehearsal necessary to retain access to the constantly fading traces of more than this number. In such circumstances, the intrusion of distracting ideation or perceptions would greatly disrupt performance. It follows that "freedom from distractibility" should result in superior performance of tasks that require the concentration of attention on a specific set of ideas.

High thalamocortical arousability lowers the threshold for memories and remote associations with the increased likelihood of greater distraction due to intruding and irrelevant ideation. In contrast, low thalamocortical arousability lowers the threshold for perception of a greater range of environmental events. In this case, there would be greater distraction due to intruding and irrelevant perceptions. Thus, the optimal condition for the concentration of attention on a specific idea, or set of ideas, is middling arousability. Moreover, because this is so, there is an exact alignment with g.

Mental Energy and g

As already noted, Spearman's ideas concerning attention were dominated by the notion that there is a mental energy analogous to physical energy, and by his important insight that something like mental energy would be required to account for the ubiquitous positive correlations between many different kinds of cognitive tests and for the g factor arising from such correlations.

While Spearman is commonly remembered for his advocacy of one general intelligence factor, this derives more from his conception of g as relating to mental energy than it does to the evidence reviewed in his account of the "abilities of man." There is actually a great deal of ambiguity in his statements concerning g. This clearly relates to a mismatch between the prediction from the mental energy concept of an all-embracing positive manifold and the actual empirical findings that he reviews.

In contrast to the mental energy concept, arousability theory explains why some aspects of cognition are related to g and others are not. In fact, it not only accounts for g but also for the other factors acknowledged by Spearman. As we have seen, it clarifies the concept of attention and details precisely how attention relates to g and to the introversion-extraversion dimension. Most significantly, with respect to Spearman's ideas, it accounts for the distinction between eduction and reproduction while explaining the close linkage between g and eduction. Equally important, it accounts for a close relationship between g and performance on discrimination tasks that in Spearman's (1904) earlier writings were regarded as the best indicators of general intelligence.

To conclude this chapter, it is noted that the three kinds of intelligence tests that have been most closely associated with g also relate in a clear and unambiguous manner to the three ways in which middling cerebral arousability enhances neural information processing. Discrimination tests evaluate the efficiency of basic neural transmission, concentration tests evaluate the efficiency of attention regulation, and eduction tests evaluate the efficiency of learning. One can reasonably claim that here again there are interesting new hypotheses for testing as well as some direct implications concerning the future construction, validation, and interpretation of general intelligence tests.

11

Freud: Insights, Errors, and New Explanations

The universality and general utility of the theory elaborated in this book has been demonstrated mainly by reference to the concepts and empirical findings of Pavlov, Eysenck, and Spearman, although, where appropriate, reference has been made to the contributions of others such as Jung, Hebb, and Cattell. In this penultimate chapter, I have gone beyond those concepts and ideas that are most closely related to the systematic measurement of individual differences. This has been done to illustrate that the new theory has a fundamental bearing on other formulations that derive from different approaches to the study of the human psyche. In this century, Freud's theory has had a more profound influence on the way people think about human nature than any other, and it is therefore to Freud that I now turn. For convenience, I will continue to refer to Freud's theory, or to psychoanalytic theory, although strictly speaking Freud was the author of a number of different theories.

Freud's psychological writings fill twenty-four volumes in the standard edition of his complete works (Freud, 1953–1974). One must assume that the quantity and literary quality of this output has done much to popularize psychoanalytic theory since the evidence for the various propositions advanced by Freud is largely anecdotal, hearsay, or in the form of *ex cathedra* pronouncements. Even allowing for Freud's forceful, persuasive, and voluminous presentation of his ideas, the kind of evidence he considers is hardly commensurable with the remarkable influence of his theory. One assumes, therefore, that this great influence is partly related to the perceived utility of the theory as an explanation for important and fundamental aspects of the human condition that are not dealt with by other theories. In short, the influence and longevity of Freud's theory can be attributed partly to its psychological relevance and partly to lack of competition.

From the foregoing, it seems likely that, despite shaky foundations, and despite frequent criticism, Freud's theory will remain a potent ideological force until it is displaced by something better. The aim here is to show that the theory developed in preceding chapters can explain the phenomena of chief interest to Freud and his successors. If this can be accomplished, the new formulation has far greater explanatory power because it already accounts for much that lies beyond the scope of psychoanalytic theory. The new formulation is also superior because it relates meaningfully to the sustained and systematic research carried on by many individuals, as distinct from the mainly casual observations and opinions of just one person. Finally, and not least important, insights provided by the new theory draw attention to some very fundamental and irremediable problems that invalidate all of the main Freudian concepts.

SUPEREGO AND ID: THE RELATIVE PREDOMINANCE OF CEREBRUM AND BRAIN STEM

As is well known, psychoanalytic theory postulates that personality is composed of three structural elements, namely, the id, ego, and superego. In essence, the id represents instinctive forces or impulses that motivate individuals to seek immediate gratification of basic biological needs and to respond with rage and aggression if such gratification is denied. In contrast, the superego represents motivational forces that inhibit the gratification of biological needs as well as the aggressive impulses that normally arise on denial of gratification.

In the Freudian formulation, the id is present from birth. The superego only develops when children identify with their parents "in order to resolve the Oedipus complex" and thereby internalize the moral values of their parents and of society. It is particularly noteworthy that the morality associated with the superego is of the negative character earlier associated with the melancholic temperament. That is to say, there is a preoccupation with ugliness and evil. Corresponding feelings of revulsion and hatred motivate criticism and censure of self and others with a general inclination to prohibit or destroy what is perceived to be evil rather than to promote or preserve what is perceived to be good.

This is not really surprising since Freud's conception of the superego was very much based on his observation of the mentally ill and especially of "melancholiacs" where, as the term implies, the traits and characteristics of melancholic individuals are present in a grossly exaggerated form. Freud's clinical observations are valuable since they emphasize how in psychiatric patients, the melancholic temperament or personality profile can in some cases be transformed almost instantly into something much more akin to that of the choleric individual. This kind of transition justifies Freud's dynamic conception of personality with different and opposed elements of personality structure competing for the control of behavior.

Freud's greatest contributions were probably the identification of the competing aspects of personality structure that he chose to describe as the superego and the id, and his recognition that mental illness is closely linked to personality and to conflicts that arise owing to an imbalance in the relative influence of these two entities. From all that has gone before, one can quite definitely and explicitly identify the superego and the id as representing the relative dominance of cerebral or brain-stem processes, respectively.

The high cerebral arousability, strong inhibition of brain-stem processes, and predominance of cortical excitation over inhibition, which have been shown earlier in this account to relate to the melancholic temperament, also determine the general psychological profile that Freud attributed to the superego. The low cerebral arousability, weak inhibition of the brain stem, and predominance of cortical inhibition over excitation, which were earlier related to the choleric temperament, also determine the general psychological profile that Freud attributed to the id. Thus we can see that the opposed structural elements of personality recognized by Freud relate essentially to the relative predominance of cerebral or brain-stem processes. In normal circumstances, the relative influence of these processes does not vary much in the case of particular individuals but may do so if, in the case of mental illness, brain damage, or some neurological disease process, the normal production and regulation of brain neurotransmitters is impaired in some way or if, as already noted, individuals ingest drugs and there are similar consequences.

THE EGO, MIDDLING CEREBRAL AROUSABILITY, AND INTELLIGENCE

To some extent, Freud's unfortunate emphasis on the pathological was ameliorated by his successors who placed far more importance on the ego and on ego development as the aim of psychotherapy and the route to psychological health. Here, again, one can demonstrate the relevance of the findings considered in earlier chapters. In the first instance, a strong ego implies a better balance between the cerebral and subcerebral influences that Freud personified as the superego and the id. This in turn implies middling cerebral arousability, but it is also explicit that a better developed ego means better or more realistic interaction with the external environment, and this implies higher intelligence.

It follows that all three Freudian components of personality structure— id, ego, and superego—can be related to the single continuum of cerebral arousability. Where, in Freudian terms, the id is dominant, there is low cerebral arousability, the choleric temperament, and lower intelligence. Where the ego is dominant, there is middling cerebral arousability, the emotional stability of either the phlegmatic or sanguine types, and high intelligence. Where the superego is dominant, there is high cerebral arousability, the melancholic temperament, and lower intelligence.

FREUD'S FLAWED CONCEPTION OF DEVELOPMENT

When Freud attributes superego development to identification with a parent, he is referring to a process of imitation or "learning by observation." A long-standing criticism of this proposition is that the superego relates to an authoritarian, prohibitive, and harshly critical moral stance that could not possibly be derived from the full range of parental attitudes and behaviors that are experienced by most children. In other words, superego development cannot truly be explained in terms of identification with a parent because one is obliged to postulate a selective acquisition of parental attitudes and behaviors that specifically excludes all of those caring behaviors and attitudes that are motivated by the great love and affection that most parents have for their children.

From the foregoing, we can see that Freud's conception of superego development quickly runs into serious difficulties, especially insofar as there is reference to learning. Things get much worse, since Freud's own observations appear to rule out any possibility that superego development could be due to learning. More specifically, the obvious conclusion to be drawn from Freud's observations concerning rapid changes in personality during the course of mental illness, or, for that matter, from knowledge of the effects of drug ingestion, is that the temperament types and the major structural aspects or dimensions of personality are not due to differences in learning experience. This is already indicated by the neurological findings described earlier, but the much more obvious point here is that while

individual learning experiences will undoubtedly influence the development of individual personalities, these cannot possibly result in two quite
distinct, comprehensive, and fully integrated personalities, one of which is
normally latent and only manifest in exceptional circumstances. Freud
failed to recognize this most important implication of his own observations.

The fundamental importance and significance of Freud's observations
are also lost on contemporary researchers such as Bandura, Mischel, and
others who first denied the existence of personality but now seek to explain
it solely or mainly in terms of learning (Bandura, 1977; Mischel, 1976).
Systematic study of the way in which human behavior is influenced by the
observation of others is clearly important, but the attempt to construct a
theory of personality based exclusively on such studies, while ignoring all
other relevant information and research, is uncomfortably akin to the
peculiar blindness and narrowness of behaviorism—a blindness and narrowness that, in Koestler's (1967) words, gave rise to the dark ages of a
psychology which denied the existence of mind, and for that matter brain,
and lived only on specious analogies derived from the bar-pressing activities of rats. Psychology cannot afford to be sidetracked yet again by the
similarly blinkered approach of those who promote "social cognitive learning theory."

Ironically, Freud's own observations concerning the vacillation of personality in the mentally ill and, in this account the linking of superego and
id with the melancholic and choleric temperaments, rules out the possibility
that the emergence of something akin to a superego is a necessary part of
normal development. Not surprisingly, Freud's clinical observations were
restricted to the emotionally unstable choleric and melancholic temperaments, and necessarily to the most extreme and pathological cases. The
fundamental causes of temperament variation have been detailed in preceding chapters, and it is clear that by drawing on his clinical observations in
order to explain normal personality, Freud equates healthy development
with progression along a continuum from the choleric temperament and an
id-like personality profile to the melancholic temperament and a superego-
like personality profile. This might be regarded as a reasonable proposition
insofar as the cerebrum exerts a progressively greater influence on brain-
stem processes during development, and one would expect some corresponding change in personality. The flaw in this thinking is that it is not at
all reasonable or acceptable to suggest that normal healthy development
and maturation will result in the emotionally unstable and otherwise less
than optimal personality profile of the melancholic.

Freud did sometimes equate psychological health with the development of a strong ego, but there is no doubt whatsoever that his explanation of moral behavior and his views concerning human achievement and the rise of civilization all relate to superego development and are manifestly erroneous in that the traits and attributes personified as the superego relate to only one of the four classical temperaments and therefore only to one of four major developmental outcomes. Through reliance on his clinical observations, the psychological profile of the melancholic, in its less extreme or "normal" form, is conceived as optimal and a model for the civilized human being. However, as we now know, such individuals lack emotional stability, they have lower IQs, and there is an exaggeration of the dark side of morality.

Since Freud's view of development from id dominance to superego dominance is manifestly inadequate, so also is his bizarre and, let us be honest, quite mad conception of children identifying with parents because they fear castration, or because they believe that this has already happened. Freud did not study children, and this is painfully evident from his pronouncements concerning the Oedipus complex, infantile sexuality, and developmental stages. These can all be rejected out of hand. Never more than conjectured embellishments, one can now see that they adorn a concept of development that is manifestly and fundamentally flawed.

Equally, we must reject Freud's conception of the differential psychological development of males and females. In this account, Oedipus has been returned to the domain of mythology. Consequently, one is no longer required to entertain the quite ridiculous notion that females are less moral than males because they lack a penis.

FREUD'S FLAWED CONCEPTION OF THE CAUSATION OF NEUROSES

Earlier, Freud was credited with the important observation that mental illness is fundamentally related to an imbalance of the structural elements of personality. These structural elements, designated by Freud as superego and id, have been identified with the relative influence and predominance of cerebral and brain-stem processes. Since this is so, we can agree with Freud that the distinction between superego and id does also involve an overlapping distinction between conscious voluntary processes (of the cerebrum) and unconscious involuntary processes (of the brain stem).

Freud believed that neurotic illness resulted from *repression* of the mental representatives of instinct and especially of ideation related to sexual impulses. When repression occurs, ideation is pushed out of consciousness and forced down into the unconscious. This, according to Freud, eventually results in neurotic illness including anxiety states, phobias, and obsessive-compulsive disorders.

An immediate difficulty here is that Freud equates mental illness with undue repression of instincts. Clearly it is equally pathological when the "instincts" dominate behavior, and this is characterized by antisocial activities, by gross self-indulgence, and by rage, aggression, and violence if gratification is delayed. In fact, Freud emphasizes processes and symptoms that can be related to the melancholic temperament but fails to deal adequately with "neuroses" that can be related to the choleric temperament.

The condition for repression to occur is that the motivational force of unpleasure due to the presence of some ideation in consciousness shall have acquired more strength than the pleasure obtained from satisfaction of the associated, and usually sexual, impulse. Sexual impulses in consciousness can be attributed to the activity of brain-stem processes, and in Freudian terms to the id. The unpleasure caused by such impulses can be related to strength of the superego but actually to the dark and prohibitive morality of the melancholic temperament. In Freudian locution, repression and the neuroses occur when the unpleasure caused by the superego is greater than the pleasure afforded by the id and when consequently sexual impulses are denied rather than gratified.

The second major problem with Freud's conception of the causation of neurotic disorder is that *one symptom of mental aberration or ill health is being used to explain another*. The fact that ideas related to the satisfaction of basic biological needs should cause revulsion and distress is already a symptom of mental illness *before* any repression of such ideas has occurred. Freud in fact observes a set of correlated symptoms and confuses correlation with causation. Anxiety states, phobias, and obsessive-compulsive behaviors can all be regarded as the exaggeration of attributes already associated with the melancholic temperament and caused by extremely high cerebral arousability and the resultant suppression of brain-stem processes and/or undue predominance of cortical excitation over inhibition. These neurological conditions can account for a wide range of somatic and psychological symptoms and disorders, including some wrongly accorded the status of causal agents by Freud.

In the most extreme cases, melancholics perceive the world as a dirty, revolting, unreliable, and evil place. They are overwhelmed and confused by overstimulation, "intruding" ideation, and probably even hallucinations, all caused by high arousability. At the same time, there is paralysis of automatic or spontaneous behaviors due to strong inhibition of brain-stem nuclei with the result that behavior relies too heavily on voluntary processes and is therefore poorly coordinated and effortful. This inhibition of brain-stem processes has other effects such as the suppression of appetite and libido, inhibition of sexual activity and digestive processes as well as sleep prevention. It is only to be expected that these problems will cause a range of secondary "symptoms" such as irrational "avoidance" and "checking" behaviors, an unusual preoccupation with matters of hygiene, and in some cases even "religious mania."

PSYCHOANALYSIS: THE ROYAL ROAD TO THE UNCONSCIOUS

If, according to Freud, the neuroses result from repression of ideation related to sexual impulses, then the cure was to burrow down into the unconscious and bring this offensive ideation back up into consciousness. Freud claimed that repressed ideation could be "detected" using psycho-analytic techniques involving either the "free association" of ideas or "dream analysis."

Psychoanalysis and Temperament Differences

Jung's version of the free-association technique involves saying the first word or associate that comes to mind following the presentation of a stimulus word. It is sometimes observed that there is a delay in providing associates for certain words and also that the reported associations are not what one might expect if the respondent were answering freely and without restraint. In the same way, free association will reveal areas of psychological experience that are not freely discussed. By omitting to provide Freud with the word associations that he expected, especially sexual ones, he would infer repression and incline towards a diagnosis of neurotic illness.

The problem here is that shy or modest people from the healthy general population would be expected to respond in this way even when there is no repression and they are perfectly aware of the sexual connotations of the presented words. Individuals in this category are likely to be introverted with above average neuroticism scores. That is to say, they would be melancholics with some inhibition of sexual behaviors and some tendency to take a prohibitive moral attitude towards sexual activity, including open discussion of sexual matters.

The fact that melancholics are ill at ease concerning sexual matters, more reserved, and less ready to divulge their innermost thoughts can be explained by predominance of cerebral over brain-stem processes and by predominance of cerebral excitation over inhibition. In extreme cases, these tendencies would be symptoms of psychopathology, but the really important point to make here is that data obtained using the free-association technique does not necessarily signify repression but perhaps only an unwillingness to discuss sexual matters. The great weakness of Freud's procedure is that one cannot tell whether material has actually been repressed or whether an individual will just not reveal certain associates that come to mind.

Some people, usually melancholics, are just not prepared to allow an analyst access to the most intimate details of their private lives. Freud's lack of insight and complete failure to understand this very elementary point is difficult to comprehend until one recalls that he was an extravert. Extraverts are not known for their reserve or modesty, and they are not subject to the sexual inhibitions and prohibitions of melancholics. Thus it can be suggested that Freud's inability to understand the reserve and modesty of melancholics led him to misinterpret the simple reluctance of such people to discuss sexual matters as the actual removal of sexual ideation from consciousness.

Freud was not always confronted with melancholics and the "dysthymic" neurotic disorders. He also encountered "hysterics" and the different neurotic disorders that can be linked to the choleric temperament. As we would expect from arousability theory, but not from Freud's account of the development of neuroses, such individuals, in contrast to melancholics, can be remarkably forthcoming about their supposed sexual experiences. I say supposed, because choleric individuals are more likely to be attention seekers and compulsive liars whose statements would definitely require independent verification.

In his dealings with hysterics, Freud again appears to be remarkably naive concerning the psychology of ordinary people, never mind those suffering mental illness. By the time he reported that he had discovered the specific cause of psychoneurotic disorder, Freud was already subjecting his patients to an aggressive cross-examination as to their sexual habits. In his retrospective accounts, Freud claimed that some of these patients reported that they had been sexually molested by one of their own parents and, believing these stories, he published his "seduction" theory of neurotic illness.

Much to Freud's embarrassment, the seduction theory came unstuck when he discovered that some of the seductions had never taken place. This embarrassment was all the greater since reviewers of his first book on hysteria had pointed to the risk that Freud's methods would cause patients to accept his "sexual" explanations for their difficulties. Thus we are left to consider whether the seduction stories were a figment of Freud's imagination or of the imagination of his patients or perhaps of both.

Freud's capacity for self-delusion, or possibly just dishonesty, is clearly revealed when the retrospective accounts of his work with hysterics are compared with the original seduction papers. As Cioffi (1974, pp. 172–173) points out, the claim that parents were the seducers "is not only not made in the original seduction papers it is inconsistent with them." Cioffi notes that "the [original] cast-list includes nursemaids, governesses, domestic servants, teachers, tutors, older children and even brothers—but no parents" (1974, p. 172). This suggests that Freud's preconceptions concerning the influence of sexual life not only invited his patients to accept a sexual cause for their difficulties but also led eventually to a "revised" version of what had been reported originally.

Through the agency of this revision, the seduction error was transformed into an important "discovery" of an infantile fantasy life and of infantile wishes for sexual relations with their parents. That is to say, the Oedipus complex was discovered, and, as is well known, this became the main source of offensive sexual ideation requiring repression and hence the main cause of neurotic disorders in psychoanalytic theory. Of course, the Oedipus complex cannot be derived from imagined seductions by just anyone. *The seducer must be a parent, and in his retrospective accounts Freud clearly revises his patients' original stories so that they can be used to justify the Oedipus concept.*

We have seen how arousability theory can explain the reticence and enthusiasm, respectively, of melancholics and cholerics in circumstances where there is an opportunity to speak of sexual matters. Notably, there is no need to refer to a process of repression, and, in any case, such a process cannot explain the different and sometimes opposite symptoms of extreme melancholics and cholerics. Equally important, the Oedipus complex appears to have arisen from Freud's imagination rather than deriving from any actual information obtained from patients concerning their supposed infantile fantasy life.

Psychoanalysis and Dreams

Freud claimed that dreams provided another means of detecting repressed mental content. He believed that the "manifest" dreams of conscious experience, the dreams that people actually recall, are transformed versions of "latent" dreams that occur in the domain of the unconscious. According to Freud, since the latent dream relates to the unconscious, and to repressed mental content, it cannot emerge directly into consciousness. It must first be disguised in various ways so that the true and psychologically painful meaning of the dream is not apparent to the dreamer. Freud claimed to have discovered the precise nature of the processes that transformed latent dreams into manifest dreams. Hence, he could also claim to be able to reconstruct the latent dreams of the unconscious from the corresponding manifest dreams that people are able to recall. In this way, he thought, one could gain access to the unconscious and to the repressed mental content causing neurotic illness.

While Freud made some very interesting observations concerning the nature of dreams, and it does seem likely that dreams can be strongly influenced by the operation of "unconscious" somatic processes, there has already been cause to reject the notion that repression causes mental illness. The view taken here is that dreams do relate in part to the activity of unconscious processes, that Freud correctly identified some characteristic features of dreams, and that knowledge of such features does indeed render dreams more comprehensible. However, all of this can be acknowledged without accepting Freud's view that repression of mental content causes mental illness and without proposing a distinction between the "manifest" dream of conscious experience and a "latent" dream of the unconscious.

One of the many anomalies of Freud's theory is that the "latent" dream of the unconscious can far more easily be regarded as the product of conscious rational processes whereas the "manifest" dream of consciousness can far more readily be attributed to the disorganized and primitive processes that one would associate with the Freudian unconscious. The need to posit two dreams and a complex process of transformation is avoided if we simply accept that the manifest dream is in fact largely the product of more primitive brain-stem processes that, during sleep, are not subject to the normal control and regulation of the cerebrum. Thus, during sleep, there can be greater activation of the cerebrum by brain-stem processes than is usually the case. Not surprisingly, dreams relate more directly and immediately to basic biological needs and unconscious somatic processes than does mental content in general.

The foregoing would account for Freud's claim that dreams very often have sexual connotations. Moreover, one would expect the sexual content of dreams to increase as a function of the degree of inhibition of sexual processes during wakefulness, just as dreaming about food is known to occur more frequently when people are fasting. This means that individuals with the maximum degree of brain-stem inhibition and therefore the least sexually active, which is to say Freud's melancholiac or dysthymic patients, would be likely to have dreams with the strongest and most lurid sexual connotations.

In this way, it is possible to understand how Freud came to link the sexual content of dreams with mental illness. However, from our new perspective, we can see that this is merely one more consequence of high cerebral arousability and the resulting pathological degree of brain-stem inhibition. That is to say, the sexual content of dreams has no *causal* significance with respect to mental illness. Equally important, frequent dreams with a strong sexual content would only be predicted for those particular neurotic and psychotic conditions that result from abnormally *high* cerebral arousability.

Mental illness can also be expected if there is abnormally low cerebral arousability and a pathologically disinhibited brain-stem. Hence there is an additional reason to reject Freud's view that mental illness is mainly caused by repression of sexual ideation. If there is abnormally low cerebral arousability, one would expect a strong influence of brain-stem processes during wakefulness with correspondingly strong sexual themes in ideation and sexually promiscuous behavior. Insofar as there is heightened sexual activity during wakefulness, and presumably more than adequate satisfaction of any basic biological need, one imagines that dreams with sexual connotations might actually occur infrequently when mental illness is caused by low cerebral arousability.

When recalled, we can agree with Freud that dreams sometimes do seem bizarre and in some respects unintelligible and that sexual connotations are not always obvious. We can go further and even acknowledge the validity of Freud's observations concerning the characteristic features of dream content and organization that allow one to distinguish dreams from the stream of conscious experience during wakefulness. However, while these features of dream content and organization do obscure the meaning of dreams, it can be suggested that this has nothing whatsoever to do with censorship or repression.

Instead, it can be argued that the unusual features of dream content and organization occur because, during sleep, the active neurological efferent systems that generate language are switched off. This is known to be so, but here it is suggested that these efferent language systems are also responsible for the organization of mental content during the waking state, and there are some quite predictable consequences when, during sleep, they are not operating.

The first expectation would be that there should be very little verbal content in dreams. This is precisely what Freud claimed. Secondly, if there is very little verbal content, we have to expect that dreams will be composed mainly in terms of a more primitive language of "visual" images. This is what Freud describes as *plastic representation*. With this more primitive language, the abstraction of possessing an object, for example, can only be represented as physically sitting down on it. Similarly, sexual activities can only be represented in terms of very concrete "visual" images or "kines-thetic" experiences.

From the foregoing, we can understand Freud's claim that his patients reported an unusually high incidence of dreams about objects such as mushrooms that look like the phallus. Rather than referring to symbolism, as Freud did, it may be suggested that in such cases the dream is about a phallus but that, on waking, the degraded pictorial image of a phallus, in an otherwise unintelligible dream, is likely to be identified as a mushroom or some other object having roughly the same physical shape.

Freud does actually refer to a process of *secondary revision* such that on waking, the brain will organize discrete elements of a dream in a way that "makes sense" but may actually distort the true meaning of the dream. This is what we might expect to happen when efferent language mechanisms are switched on again and must organize the residual mental content that is left over from sleep. The same process of secondary revision would be expected to label the image of a phallus as a mushroom or some other object that is more frequently encountered in normal waking experience.

The disorganization of dream content is also described by Freud in terms of *condensation* and *displacement*. Condensation is the term Freud coined to describe the characteristic "shorthand" nature of dream sequences with bits left out and with similar elements fused or reduced to just one element. By displacement, Freud meant allusion in dreams, where "ideas" are often represented in a remote or indirect fashion. Displacement also refers to a shifting of emphasis in dreams away from the important to the unimportant. Clearly, Freud's condensation and displacement are also exactly the kind of features we would expect in dreams when mental content is not being organized and structured by the operation of active efferent language systems.

To conclude, it is suggested that Freud made some interesting and probably valid observations concerning the content and organization of dreams. However, these observations can be understood in terms of the balance of cerebral and brain-stem processes and in terms of the absence of organization of mental content during dreaming that is normally imposed by efferent language systems. From this perspective, there are very good additional grounds for rejecting the notion that "repression of sexual ideation" causes mental illness or that the unintelligible nature of dreams is in any way related to repression or censorship.

FREUD'S FLAWED CONCEPTION OF MORALITY

Freud's extremely dismal conception of the human psyche clearly and directly derives from his involvement with extreme and pathological examples of the melancholic and choleric temperaments. This is lucidly brought out when he responds to the criticism that a human is not merely a sexual being but has nobler and higher feelings. According to Freud, the starting point for his work was the symptom; and from the symptom, the path of psychoanalysis led to the unconscious, to the life of the instincts, and to sexuality. His response to the criticism of undue emphasis on human sexuality was simply that he had to consider the instincts first, and it took time before he could turn his attention to the ego of popular psychology and to consideration of the nobler and higher feelings. From his lecture on the dissection of the psychical personality, one can see just how consideration of extreme and pathological instances of the melancholic temperament led to Freud's conception of the higher and nobler feelings of humanity.

According to Freud, pathology, with its magnification and exaggeration, can make us aware of normal phenomena that we might otherwise overlook. This is undoubtedly so, but one must also add the caution that the study of pathological conditions may also lead, as in this case, to a completely incorrect and distorted view of the normal condition. Freud uses the analogy of the crystal that, thrown to the ground, will shatter into fragments. However, this does not happen in haphazard fashion, since the shape of the fragments is determined by the normally invisible structure of the crystal. Freud suggests that psychotics are fissured and splintered structures, such as these, where the normally invisible components or elements of personality are revealed as distinct and separate entities.

The clinical picture, he claims, throws into sharp relief the severity and even cruelty of the superego function and the vicissitudes through which its relations with the ego may pass. He refers to the condition of the melancholic and especially to the pathological, exaggerated, and sometimes transient manifestation of this temperament. He points to the remarkable way in which the superego treats the ego. During an attack, the superego becomes oversevere, abuses, humiliates, and illtreats the unfortunate ego, threatens it with punishments, and reproaches it for long forgotten actions.

The most severe moral standards are applied, and here one must stress that the morality in question involves feelings of loathing, revulsion, and hatred evoked by persons, including the self, objects, and behaviors perceived to be ugly, unclean, and evil.

As Freud points out, it is a remarkable experience to observe morality functioning as a periodic phenomenon. In some cases, after a number of months, the whole moral fuss comes to an end, the critical voice of the superego is silent, and something exactly the reverse takes place. The ego finds itself in an ecstatic state of exaltation and gives itself up in an uninhibited fashion to the satisfaction of all its desires. Here, of course, the contrast is simply an exaggerated reflection of the normal distinction between the melancholic and choleric temperaments.

Such conditions are indeed revealing, as Freud claims, and in this account they are attributed to a breakdown of the mechanisms that in normal individuals regulate cerebral arousability and the balance of excitatory and inhibitory neurotransmitters. It is unfortunate however that Freud was led to equate the "higher and nobler feelings" with the operation of a deranged perceptual and emotional system that exaggerates the perception of ugliness and evil and amplifies feelings of loathing, disgust, and hatred. Equally disastrous is the omission of any reference to the moral force of the human capacity to love and seek to preserve what is perceived to be beautiful and good.

It remains to point out that Freud's failure to recognize the importance of individual differences led to the break with Jung and to Jung's work on psychological types (Jung, 1971). This offers a far less pessimistic view of the human condition, and although Jung does not acknowledge a link between the classical temperaments and his introverted and extraverted types, it can now be asserted that this is indeed the case, even if the classical descriptions of temperament emphasized affect rather than mind and attitudes of consciousness. No student of personality or individual differences should fail to read Jung's work because, more than any other, it reveals the great general significance of temperament differences with respect to human culture and intellectual activities.

The failure of Freud's theory to deal adequately with the "higher and nobler" feelings and aspirations of humanity, a problem already identified by the "humanist" psychologists (Maslow, 1968; Rogers, 1980), can now be understood in simple terms as a failure to know and understand the psychologies of the sanguine and phlegmatic temperaments. An understanding of the sanguine type is especially important. Here also there is a lopsided morality, but one can see in sharp relief how behavior is motivated by the moral force of love rather than hatred and by the ability to perceive "goodness" as distinct from "evil."

The implications of new insights concerning the role of "cerebral" emotions are of such central importance for any attempt to understand the human condition that these will be discussed further in the next and final chapter. In this concluding chapter, some general implications of the new theory are discussed. These bear on fundamental philosophical questions and offer a new perspective on human nature.

12

Human Nature and the Human Predicament

As noted earlier, the neurological parameters described in this account are likely to be altered by any environmental factor, such as brain damage, that can alter normal CNS function. On the other hand, it is difficult to suggest how, under normal circumstances, such parameters might be altered by learning. The implication here is that individual differences in the healthy general population are largely the result of genotype variation. This implication is confirmed by the results of twin studies which indicate strong genetic determination, not only of the psychological correlates of the neurological parameters, but also of related neurological variables such as the midfrequency of EEG alpha activity.

TWIN STUDIES AND GENETIC ENDOWMENT

Twin studies have stimulated a great deal of argument and debate that has most often centered on the heritability of intelligence or IQ. Although the results of such studies demonstrate consistently that IQ differences are mostly due to genotype variation, there is much opposition to acceptance of these findings. This is hardly surprising since the enormous political significance of any conclusion favoring either nature or nurture is very obvious, and there are always those who prefer to shoot the messenger than permit any challenge to a cherished political dogma. However, while it is unfortunate that the nature versus nurture debate confounds political and

scientific objectives, something useful does derive from ideologically motivated opposition and criticism in that twin studies have become increasingly more sophisticated and rigorous. This is especially true of the most
recent and ongoing study conducted by the Minnesota Center for Twin and
Adoption Research, where the results essentially confirm those reported by
earlier investigators.

The study of twins reared apart provides the simplest and most powerful
method for untangling the relative influence of genetic and environmental
factors on human individual differences. The Minnesota Study of Twins
Reared Apart began in 1979, and, since then, over 100 sets of twins have
participated. Because twins reared apart are something of a rarity, previous
studies capitalizing on this important circumstance are few in number and
limited in terms of the number of twin pairs studied. In the Minnesota study,
unprecedented energy and initiative has been employed to locate reared-
apart twin pairs in the United States, Australia, Canada, China, New
Zealand, Sweden, and West Germany and to bring them to the Minnesota
Center. In what is undoubtedly the most comprehensive study of human
individual differences ever undertaken, participants complete approximately fifty hours of medical and psychological assessment, including
measures of the core psychological differences described in earlier chapters.

The strategy of the reared-apart twin study is essentially simple, although
some complex models and statistical procedures can be employed for data
analysis. In the reared-apart study, one can evaluate the "effect" on specified
characteristics of having identical genes (MZ twins) with either the same
family environment or different family environments. The effect of having
less genetic similarity (e.g., DZ twins) can also be observed and again with
either the same family environment or different family environments. For
the IQ and personality measures of interest here, it has been found that while
scores vary from one twin pair to another, much as they do from one
individual to another in the general population, there is remarkably little
difference in the scores obtained by members of twin pairs with identical
genes; *even when these twins are reared apart in different family environments*. In addition, it transpires that the reduced genetic similarity of
nonidentical twins is accompanied by less similar IQ and personality scores
while variation in the degree of similarity of the family environment has no
appreciable influence on scores. The results of the Minnesota study, consistent with earlier findings, indicate that the IQ and personality differences
of interest in this account are usually, and in large measure, caused by
genetic differences.

Bouchard and his associates state that "study of these reared-apart twins has led to two general and seemingly remarkable conclusions concerning the sources of psychological differences—or behavioral variation—between people: (I) genetic factors have a pronounced and pervasive influence on behavioral variability, and (II) the effect of being reared in the same home is negligible for many psychological traits" (Bouchard, Lykken, McGue, Segal, and Tellegen, 1990, p. 223).

From their own study and three earlier studies of twins reared apart, these investigators estimate that *in adults* genetic factors account for approximately 70% of IQ variance. For the personality measures employed in their study, approximately 50% of the variance was attributable to genetic factors. In both cases, these estimates are attenuated by measurement error, but it should also be noted that the relatively narrow, "trait-oriented" personality scales used in the Minnesota study would be more sensitive to the effects of individual learning experiences than the measures of broad, "higher-order" personality dimensions developed by the Eysencks. Moreover, the particular personality scales used in the Minnesota study would not be expected to reflect neurological and genetic differences as well as those developed by the Eysencks and explicitly related to a theory of cerebral arousability.

Bouchard and his associates acknowledge that these results and conclusions will not surprise other behavioral geneticists who have observed similar results and drawn similar conclusions (e.g., Eaves, Eysenck, and Martin, 1989; Plomin and Daniels, 1987). However, as they point out, this study and the broader behavioral genetic literature challenge prevailing psychological theories on the origins of individual differences in ability, personality, interests, and social attitudes.

Bouchard et al. (1990) go on to point out that while naturalists and animal breeders are aware of the wide and heritable differences in behavior of other species,

there is a curious reluctance among some scientists (Lewontin, Rose and Kamin, 1984) to acknowledge the contribution of genetic variation to psychological differences within the human species. Our findings support and extend those from many family, twin and adoption studies (Loehlin, 1989; Plomin and Loehlin, 1989), a broad consilience of findings leading to the following generalizations: For almost every behavioral trait so far investigated, from reaction time to religiosity, an important fraction of the variation among people turns out to be associated with genetic variation. This fact need no longer be subject to debate (Scarr, 1987); rather, it is time to consider its implications. (227)

An important caveat introduced by Bouchard et al., and strongly endorsed by me, is that the IQ heritability estimate of 70% should not be extrapolated to the extremes of environmental disadvantage, encountered even in "developed" societies, since these extremes are not well represented in twin samples. Moreover, the 70% estimate is not a figure that relates to individuals. It is an average value across individuals which applies only to the broad middle class in developed societies such as the United States and only to current environmental circumstances.

The point is also made that parents could obviously produce shared family effects if they grossly deprived or mistreated all their children. Likewise, Bouchard and his associates acknowledge that charismatic parents, determined to make all their children share certain personal qualities, interests, or values, might sometimes succeed. The remarkable similarity in social attitudes such as traditionalism and religiosity of identical twins reared apart does not show that parents cannot influence these traits but simply that *this does not tend to happen in most families.*

Finally, Bouchard et al. suggest that the specific mechanisms by which genetic differences are expressed in phenotypic differences are largely unknown. This is where the findings described in earlier chapters complement those obtained in twin studies and where the value of the new theory mapped out in earlier chapters can again be demonstrated. If twin studies reveal a relationship between the first and last links of an unknown causal chain, then the new theory traces out the causal sequence that connects these links.

For example, in the case of IQ, we can say that genetic differences cause differences in cerebral arousability. In turn, these differences cause differences in the neurological systems of information transmission, of attention regulation and recall, and of learning. In all three cases, middling arousability is optimal, and this ensures that there is the "positive manifold" of correlated abilities that gives rise to the concept of general intelligence and IQ. Thus, when an individual performs well on one cognitive task, performance is also likely to be above average on other tasks that do not appear to be related to the first task in any obvious way.

Because of the threefold manner in which general intelligence is determined, one would expect that measures of sensory discrimination, measures of attention regulation, and measures of the capacity to educe relations and correlates would all be especially good markers of general intelligence. As we saw earlier, the literature suggests that this is indeed the case. Also, as explained earlier, one can account for both the single general intelligence factor identified by Spearman and for the three correlated general intelligence factors identified by Cattell and Horn.

In similar fashion, one can trace out the missing links in the causal chain leading from genetic differences to personality differences. There is the additional bonus here that the interrelatedness of the causal chains for intelligence and personality accounts for the discovery of meaningful relationships between intelligence, personality, and temperament variables. Thus, while the Minnesota study and the broader behavioral genetic literature challenge prevailing psychological theories, there is strong support for the new theory described in preceding chapters. It is particularly significant that the new theory explains not only intelligence and personality differences but can also account for the genetically determined differences in social and moral attitudes that behavior geneticists find most puzzling and incomprehensible. In this particular domain, there are such profound and startling implications concerning the nature of the human condition that some further discussion seems obligatory.

GENES, ARCHETYPES, CEREBRAL EMOTIONS, AND MORALITY

Freud's observations concerning the periodicity of morality in mental illness, the transient changes in personality and moral attitudes caused by drug ingestion, and, earlier in this account, the linking of morality with the relative predominance of cerebral inhibitory and excitatory transmitter substances all raise difficult questions and appear to devalue much that human beings consider to be fundamentally important. As Freud noted, people often think of morality as something conferred on them by God. It is an article of faith for many people of different religious persuasions that God endowed human beings with the capacity to discriminate right from wrong, beauty from ugliness, and good from evil.

Strange as it may seem, the Bible does not actually tell us unequivocally that morality was God given. At the beginning of Genesis, it is the serpent, not God, who persuades Eve to eat the fruit of the tree of knowledge. God had warned Adam and Eve not to eat this fruit, "lest you die." The serpent told Eve that they would not die: "For God knows well the moment that you eat of it your eyes shall be opened and you will be like gods who know what is good and what is bad" (Gen. 3:5 New American Bible).

Eve was tempted to eat the fruit not only because she saw that it was good for food and pleasant to the eyes but also because it was "a tree . . . desirable for gaining wisdom" (Gen. 3:6 NAB). On eating the fruit, "the eyes of both of them were opened and they realized that they were naked" (Gen.

3:7 NAB). When God discovered that they knew of their nakedness, he banished Adam and Eve from Eden saying: "See! The man has become like one of us, knowing what is good and what is bad! Therefore, he must not be allowed to put out his hand to take fruit from the tree of life also, and thus eat of it, and live forever [he must be sent forth from Eden]" (Gen. 3:22 NAB).

In this biblical story, morality is not a gift from God, but it is clear that the ancients equated knowledge of good and evil with divine wisdom and regarded this as the particular quality that sets humankind apart from other creatures. In opposition to such views, are we now to believe that our capacity for aesthetic appreciation, our moral sense, and indeed the underpinning of the whole system of human motives and values derives solely from the particular mix of neurotransmitters with which we are endowed?

Such a conclusion would be too simplistic, but it is impossible to deny the importance of the mix of neurotransmitters. These do cause profound differences in the way that ordinary people think, feel, and act. If the mix deviates sufficiently from normal, we know that people become insane. However, discrimination of good and evil does not depend fundamentally on the imbalance of excitatory and inhibitory neurotransmitters that renders melancholics generally more responsive to "evil" and sanguine individuals generally more responsive to "goodness." All that these differences reveal is that particular cerebral neurotransmitters mediate particular emotional responses and that it is meaningful to refer to higher cerebral emotions of love and hate that motivate moral behavior.

If one accepts that humanity has evolved not just greater intellectual capacity but also a greater capacity for emotional experience, we are still left with the difficult problem of explaining why particular events evoke the emotion of love whereas others evoke hatred. There is a similar problem when we try to explain why particular patterns of sensory stimulation are perceived as beautiful whereas others are considered ugly. Through learning we can become better able to perceive the intricacies of a pattern but, finally, learning has nothing whatsoever to do with our experience of the pattern as ugly or beautiful. Similarly, the capacity to experience the emotion of love is not learned; it is merely triggered in a predetermined fashion by some events but not by others.

Difficult though it is to accept, the only explanation that seems feasible is that evolution not only increased the range of emotional experiences but also determined a preparedness to respond emotionally in a particular fashion to quite complex events. This notion was introduced earlier when the idea of higher cerebral emotions was first proposed. As noted then, it is actually a restatement of Jung's theory of archetypes when one claims that contemporary events or circumstances can unlock powerful, self-transcending emotions that motivate behavior in accordance with stereotyped event-emotion-behavior patterns. These patterns are determined by natural selection and relate to behaviors that had "good" or "bad" consequences for our ancestors. As a result, the higher, self-transcending, cerebral emotions must be accorded a status at least equal to intellect in the determination of behavior that is characteristically human.

It seems reasonable to propose that the cerebral emotions are triggered by environmental events or circumstances that, during the last period of evolutionary development, were linked in some way to the welfare of small social groups and where behaviors motivated by these emotions could increase the likelihood that the community would survive and prosper. One concludes, like Jung, that there is a range of environmental events, circumstances, or symbols that have the capacity to trigger the emotions of love and hate together with associated behavioral tendencies. These genetically determined event-emotion-behavior relationships constitute the wisdom of the ages, and they would appear to be the source of all moral and aesthetic knowledge.

Freud grappled with the question of morality, but as we saw in an earlier chapter, his lopsided formulation only dealt with hatred of evil. Here, as elsewhere, we do not have a satisfactory account of the origin of moral attitudes and moral behavior. In Freudian theory, morality comes from the parents who got it from their parents and so on. This only presents us with an infinite regression and fails to answer the question of primary interest.

Morality is very often the special concern of religious institutions. In this context, God is usually regarded as the source of moral laws. In the domain of science, this is not very helpful, and especially so when we are faced with some obvious contradictions and inconsistencies. In the Bible, for example, we are first told that God did not want Adam and Eve to know the difference between right and wrong and that moral knowledge came to us instantly and completely through the forbidden fruit and the good offices of the serpent. Later on, it appears that this was not lasting or effective and that God has a change of heart, because he writes out the moral laws on stone tablets and gives them to Moses. In this latter account, humankind is no longer endowed with divine wisdom but must learn off some rules of conduct the hard way. In fact, morality is often regarded as just some rule or habit of conduct that refers to standards of right and wrong. Alternatively, reference might be made to a set of customs in a given society which regulate relationships and prescribe modes of behavior to enhance the group's survival. These definitions are quite inadequate since there is no reference to the central role and motivating force of emotions, just as there is no explanation of the origin of such codes. In every human society, people have tried to give expression to their innate knowledge of good and evil, but the codification of this ancient genetic wisdom could never result in any absolutely clear-cut set of rules or standards of right and wrong.

The codes that are produced certainly have common and overlapping themes, but they are subject to the vagaries of time, place, and circumstance. They would also differ quite radically if formulated by different temperament types. If a society is dominated by choleric types, one would expect less emphasis on morality and the motivating power of cerebral emotions. Instead behavior would be understood more in terms of hedonism and self-interest with motivation provided by the kind of mechanistic pursuit of pleasure and avoidance of pain that underpins contemporary behaviorism. Where the sanguine and melancholic types have a dominant influence, there would be well-developed moral codes but these would emphasize "loving God" and "hating the Devil," respectively. For example, we can infer that the authors of the Old Testament were more likely to have had the melancholic temperament, which emphasizes the emotion of hate and the destruction of evil. In contrast, the life and death of Jesus Christ is a testament to the power of love, and the whole emphasis in Christ's teaching is on loving and forgiving.

There are many ways in which dominance of particular temperament types would influence society. For example, in medieval Europe, people lived in the age of the melancholic temperament where the dominant influence of the Church and of those of a religious inclination was everywhere evident. Today, in the West, and especially in the United States, we live in an age of extraversion. By contrasting these two periods in history, one can begin to appreciate just how much differences in temperament can affect a culture. The view taken here is that logical as well as empirical considerations force one to conclude that people create cultures, and it is only in a superficial and secondary sense that cultures create people. From this discussion, it would follow that while we may legitimately speak of human values that come to us as part of our genetic endowment, we must also accept that for each temperament type, the relative weightings of these values will differ. These values may be awakened by appropriate experiences and examples, and they may be sharpened and refined by education, but the evidence being accumulated by behavioral geneticists now requires rejection of the "selfish-gene" proposal and any suggestion that self-transcending behavior is merely or fundamentally a product of culture and learning (Dawkins, 1976). Even in the absence of such evidence, one marvels that a whole book of speculative arguments could be written in support of the selfish-gene notion when it is axiomatic that altruistic behaviors are motivated by the emotion of love and that the *quality* of emotional experiences, and the *derivative character* of corresponding behaviors, just cannot be explained in terms of learning.

INTELLIGENCE, MORALITY, AND HEDONISM: THE LEGACY AND THE APOCALYPSE

One of the major criticisms of the dominant contemporary theories of psychology is that they do not help us to understand the human predicament, and worse, that they actually constitute part of the problem. This is particularly true in the case of behaviorism, and even now one must agree with Koestler (1967) when he states that the Watson-Hull-Skinner tradition is still immensely powerful and that it still keeps an invisible stranglehold on academic psychology. Koestler concludes his criticism of behaviorism with a quotation from von Bertalanffy (1967) which drives home this point and illustrates the awful inadequacy of existing psychological theories while drawing attention to the way in which behaviorism in particular continues to dehumanize people. It is fitting that I should reproduce this quotation here:

Let us face the fact: a large part of modern psychology is a sterile and pompous scholasticism which, with the blinkers of preconceived notions or superstitions, doesn't see the obvious; which covers the triviality of its results and ideas with a preposterous language bearing no resemblance to normal English or sound theory, and which provides modern society with the techniques for the progressive stultification of mankind. It has been justly said that American positivist philosophy—and the same even more applies to psychology—has achieved the rare feat of being both extremely boring and frivolous in its unconcern with human issues. . . .

I don't care a jot whether [psychologists] have modified Watson, Hull and Freud here and there and have replaced their blunt statements by more qualified and sophisticated circumlocutions. I do care a lot that the spirit is still all-pervading in our society; reducing man to the lower aspects of his animal nature, manipulating him into a feeble-minded automaton of consumption or a marionette of political power, systematically stultifying him by a perverse system of education, in short, dehumanizing him ever farther by means of a sophisticated psychological technology.

It is the expressed or implicit contention that there is no essential difference between rat and man which makes American psychology so profoundly disturbing. *"When the intellectual elite, the thinkers and leaders, see in man nothing but an overgrown rat, then it is time to be alarmed*" (von Bertalanffy, cited by Koestler, 1967, pp. 352 –353, emphasis added).

Clearly, any valid theory of psychology ought to have a direct bearing on the most fundamental issues and problems that confront humanity, but the most influential contemporary theories of psychology do not pass this elementary test. In the last pages of this account, I will seek to demonstrate that the theory formulated in preceding chapters does have a direct bearing on the nature of the human predicament. I will also suggest that it helps us to understand the true nature of humanity and thereby provides a formula for survival in the future. In *The Evolution of Human Nature*, Judson Herrick (1971) states that

[the] history of civilization is a record of slow but dramatic enrichment of human life interspersed with episodes of wanton destruction of all the accumulated riches of property and spiritual values. These episodic reversions to bestiality seem to be increasing in virulence and in the magnitude of the resulting disasters until now we are threatened with the loss of everything that has been won in our struggle for the better life. (398)

Here one must question the suggestion that the wanton destructiveness of humans is a "reversion to bestiality" if only because there is nothing remotely comparable in the behavior of other animals and because the facts imply a progressive rather than a regressive degeneration. Also, with each day that passes, there is fresh evidence of the great harm that has been done to our planet in the struggle for a "better life." A great American corporation once used the motto "better things for better living through chemistry." It is, perhaps, a reflection of the times in which we live that this motto is no longer used.

In this account, I need not catalogue all the specific social and environmental problems that threaten to overwhelm humanity, but I do want to suggest that the cause of many such difficulties is related to what Herrick describes as the "tumorous overgrowth" of the human brain. Koestler (1967, p. 272) takes up this general idea when he examines the notion that there might be a constructional fault inside the human skull that threatens us with eventual extinction. He refers to an article by Le Gros Clark who claims that the first reason for such a suspicion is the extraordinary rapidity of the evolutionary growth of the human brain. According to Le Gros Clark, the fossil record shows that from the middle Pleistocene, about half a million years ago, the human brain entered a phase of "explosive evolution" and expanded at a remarkable speed, "greatly exceeding the rate of evolutionary change recorded for any anatomical character in lower animals" (Le Gros Clark, cited by Koestler, 1967, p. 272).

Drawing heavily on the research and ideas of Professor Paul MacLean, Koestler suggests that it is not actually the increased size of the brain that causes problems for humankind, but rather it is poor coordination between phylogenetically old areas of the brain, and the new, specifically human areas, which were superimposed on it with such unseemly haste. According to Koestler, the consequences of this innate "schizophysiology" range from the creative to the pathological. Forms of pathology vary from what we regard as more or less normal behavior, where unconscious emotional bias distorts reasoning only to a moderate extent, in socially approved or tolerated ways, through the open smoldering conflicts of neurosis, to psychosis and psychosomatic disease. It is clear from this account that Koestler's analysis leads to conclusions concerning human individual differences that foreshadow the findings described in earlier chapters linking predominance of the cerebrum with the melancholic temperament and predominance of brain-stem processes with the choleric temperament.

There is a further parallel when Koestler makes a corresponding distinction between self-transcending and self-assertive behaviors. The latter would relate to the primary aggression of individuals, but, according to Koestler, this is not the cause of the evils of humankind. Rather, he claims, the evils of humankind result from *self-transcending identification with groups* whose common denomination is low intelligence and high emotionality. This leads to the conclusion that the delusional streak running through history is not due to individual forms of lunacy, but to the collective delusions generated by emotion-based belief systems.

I clearly cannot disagree with Koestler's argument that an imbalance of cerebral and subcerebral brain systems can cause individual lunacy and that growth of the cerebrum is related to the appearance of integrative and self-transcending behaviors related to group identification. Nor would I disagree that these contribute to human suffering, individually in the case of crime and mental illness, and collectively in the case of group conflict and war. However, although Koestler's analysis takes him a long way towards understanding the problem, he still fails to grasp the essential nature and full extent of the difficulties facing humanity.

Here it is proposed that the *fundamental* problem does not derive from a lack of coordination or balance between old and new brain structures. This lack of coordination does occur in some individuals, and in the theory here formulated, it lies at the heart of psychological conflict, neurosis, and psychosis. It may also exacerbate the major problems of humanity, but it is not the main or fundamental cause of such problems. *Instead, it is suggested that with the explosive development of the cerebrum in recent prehistory, there was a great increase in general intelligence and also a great increase in the influence of the self-transcending cerebral emotions, love and hate. The human predicament arises as a direct but delayed consequence of this increased intelligence and of the increased influence of the cerebral emotions.*

It is widely accepted that the development of a larger brain in *homo sapiens* resulted in a greatly enhanced intellectual capacity. Some anthropologists have reservations on this point since one would also expect a correlation between brain size and intelligence within species, and, it is claimed, this has not been demonstrated. For example, Henneberg writes that "within the only presently living hominid species there is virtually no correlation between mental capacity and brain size" (1987, p. 215). In fact, as Lynn (1990) points out, there are at least ten reports in the literature that consistently demonstrate a low positive correlation between indices of brain size and intelligence measures. The correlation coefficients reported in these earlier studies ranged from +0.10 to +0.35, and Lynn confirms correlations of this order in two separate studies. According to Lynn, "the evidence is sufficiently strong to make it indisputable that brain size and intelligence in man are significantly positively associated" and that "this conclusion allows us to adopt the obvious explanation for the rapid evolution of brain size in the hominids" (1990, p. 243).

The obvious explanation is simply that larger brains increased intelligence and thereby conferred a selection advantage. A relatively small correlation between brain-size indices and intelligence in humans does not in any way conflict with the findings reviewed earlier even if such a correlation related to factors not so far discussed. However, it transpires that such a correlation can be predicted from theory since the increase in mammalian brain size relative to body weight, and the even more dramatic threefold increase in hominid brain size during recent prehistory, does not signify a *general* increase in the size of all brain structures or subsystems. In fact, the increased size of mammalian and hominid brains is generally attributed to the development of the neocortex and a corresponding enlargement of the cerebrum.

In terms of the theory worked out in preceding chapters, this implies not just an increase in general intelligence or an increase in "associative power" due to greater numbers of neurons, but, in hominids at least, it implies the appearance of all those traits and abilities noted earlier that relate to predominance of cerebral over brain-stem processes. Significantly, these would include verbal abilities, greater behavioral inhibition, and greater control of behavior by ideation. From this we can conclude that the increasing relative size of the cerebrum during hominid evolution is analogous to the effect of increasing arousability when arousability is still below the optimal level. In both cases, the relative influence of the cerebrum varies, but in one instance this results from structural changes whereas, in the other, it results from functional changes. Further, it is clear that there is no inconsistency in claiming that increased intelligence during hominid development was mainly due to growth of the cerebrum whereas contemporary individual differences in human intelligence are mainly due to differences in cerebral arousability.

It would be strange indeed if the selection pressures that forced the explosive development of the cerebrum, and a whole spectrum of related and equally dramatic psychological developments, did not cause some refinement and development of the capacity for emotional experience. Such refinement and development of the capacity for emotional experience would account for the observation that people are motivated to engage in a far wider range of activities and behaviors than those of infrahuman species. That is to say, it is not enough to say that people have the intellectual capacity to learn and perform such behaviors, one must also explain the motivation. Freud attempted to do this in terms of cultural influence, development of the superego, and "sublimation" of sexual energy. Freud's account of development has already been rejected, and here a simpler, more direct explanation is proposed.

In a prior publication, I have suggested that intelligence, more than any other attribute, distinguishes and elevates the human species. On reflection, I now retract that statement. The general ability of people does far exceed that of other species, but it is not what we can do that elevates and ennobles humanity; it is why we do it. The emotion of love causes people to look beyond themselves and act unselfishly for the greater good. This emotion, above all, elevates and ennobles humanity and perhaps the greatest example of its power and motive force is given to us in the life and death of Christ. The emotion of hate is also self-transcending. Hitler provides a good illustration of its power and motive force, not only as an individual but also by the manner in which he used emotion to motivate a nation. If Christ is an exemplar of the sanguine temperament, Hitler is an exemplar of the melancholic. In both cases, these individuals were able to touch the emotional core of humanity and unlock enormous motivational forces. In both cases, they paid the ultimate penalty demanded by the self-transcending emotions.

The great mistake made by earlier writers in considering the role of emotion was to regard this as something we have in common with infrahuman species, a kind of psychological appendix that we inherited from our infrahuman ancestors and one that impairs our capacity to make full use of the new intellectual power that we have acquired. In fact, the cerebral emotions appear to have been acquired by humans in the very recent past and during the same period of explosive cerebral growth that gave us higher general intelligence. The emotions of love and hate have been too infrequently considered by psychologists but hopefully, in this account, it has been possible to demonstrate that they are closely related to the moral values and self-transcending behaviors that most people would regard as the very essence of humanity.

As already noted, we cannot account for the great achievements of humanity merely by reference to intelligence. Intelligence only ever achieves anything in the service of emotion, and all behavior is motivated by emotion. The original value of the self-transcending emotions seems clear. They enabled individuals to live successfully in social groups by motivating behaviors that placed the welfare of the group above the welfare of the individual. More specifically, one can say that they motivated individuals to identify with a group and to preserve what is good for that group in the social and material environment while prohibiting or destroying what is bad for the group. Good and bad are determined by the past experience of the species and, most immediately, by the genetic endowment of the individual.

By their nature, these self-transcending emotions motivate a far wider range of behaviors than those related to satisfaction of basic biological needs. They are intimately associated with aesthetic appreciation and an increased interest in the intrinsic qualities of people and things in the environment, an interest that is clearly revealed by the cave paintings of early humans. Thus, it is the marriage of higher intelligence and the externally directed motive force of the self-transcending emotions that account for the spectacular success and achievements of humanity and for our peculiarly human attributes. However, this same marriage has less immediate and, until recent times less obvious, delayed consequences. These delayed consequences threaten the demise of humanity and the death of our planet.

With the acquisition of high intelligence and the cerebral emotions, humankind was no longer a passive plaything of environmental forces. For the first time, a living organism acquired the capacity to actively and consciously alter the environment. The advantages were immediate and obvious as humankind moved into the era of agriculture and then, recently, with an ever-quickening tempo of technical innovation, into the industrial era. These wealth-producing activities and related developments supported an exponential population growth and led to the urbanization of a large proportion of the human population. Belatedly, we are beginning to realize that the very profound environmental changes wrought by humankind, sometimes deliberately, but often unwittingly, have disastrous long-term consequences.

The environmental changes fall into two major categories. First, we have changed the material environment. This includes not only the introduction of "pollutants" to atmosphere, soil, and oceans but also the construction of artificial "concrete" environments as well as the wholesale destruction of flora and fauna. Ultimately, we have succeeded in altering the worldwide climate in a way that will have cataclysmic and possibly disastrous consequences. Less dramatically, many millions of people currently live in misery with increasingly poor physical and psychological health as the material environment becomes increasingly toxic.

The second category of environmental change concerns the social environment. It is clear that humanity evolved to live in the particular social environment that we can associate with small nomadic groups of hunter-gatherers. With the application of intelligence to the development of technology and agriculture, there was a radical change in the nature of the social environment. Population density increased and people started to live in larger, static groups. The accumulation of wealth meant that some individuals could acquire correspondingly great power over other members of the community. To exercise this power, and to protect the wealth that made it possible, it was necessary to recruit armed guards. Inevitably, with different groups now living in close proximity and claiming ownership of land, there are territorial disputes and tribal battles.

Ultimately, of course, we have the rise of great states with correspondingly powerful armed forces that now possess weapons of mass destruction. In this century, humankind has waged war on a scale unparalleled in the whole period of recorded history and, as we all know, weapons now exist that could easily annihilate the whole planet. In the first instance, warfare and the unequaled destructive capacity of humans can be related directly to changes in our social environment that render the cerebral emotions inappropriate. That is to say, the cerebral emotions are appropriate in the context of small, widely dispersed groups of hunter-gatherers. In this context, they motivate behaviors that aid survival. The emotion of love motivates behavior that preserves what is good for the survival of the community. The emotion of hate motivates behavior that prohibits or destroys what is bad for the survival of the community. With increased population density and the close proximity of different competing groups, the emotion of hate is inappropriately and increasingly responsible for the destruction of other human beings. *That is to say, our genetically determined emotions and related behaviors are no longer appropriate when we alter the environment within which the corresponding genes were acquired.*

Today, as we enter an era that may be the catastasis of the great drama of life, the social environment in large cities has changed so dramatically that there is often no identifiable community nor any vestige of traditional family life. Socially, as well as materially, we live in an increasingly alien and hostile environment. The tragedy is that, collectively, if not individually, it is an environment of our own making. If we wish to achieve the optimal conditions for human existence, it is clear that we must seek to restore the kind of "natural" material and social environment experienced by early humans. This, of course, could only be an exceptionally long-term goal, but if humanity is to survive, and perhaps even return to Eden, it is a goal that must be pursued with relentless and single-minded determination.

Although the theory described in this book is first and foremost concerned with personality differences or, more specifically, with temperament and intelligence differences, it must now be clear that it also bears on the most profound issues and questions concerning the spiritual life of humanity. In particular, it is suggested that human genes are the primary source and the fountainhead of all human spiritual values. It might appear from this statement that humanity has suddenly been devalued. This is not so since whatever existed before remains unchanged and its value has not been altered. However, every individual can now lay claim to an intrinsic, noble nature and state with assurance that men and women are not just straws to be blown this way or that way in accordance with contemporary circumstances. Humanity is the supreme achievement of life, and the fruits of that record of achievement are no less holy or divine because they are handed down to us in our genetic endowment.

With this new emphasis on genetic endowment, it might seem that the spiritual nature of humankind can be accounted for without reference to a deity or to any supernatural domain. This is not so, since we still cannot explain the quality of subjective experience nor the phenomenon of life in terms of natural science. Even if one can point to the manner in which genes determine spiritual values, morality, religiosity, and religion, this does not really answer the key question concerning human existence. It does not explain the origin of life, and it does not tell us whether life is the product of some divine plan or purpose. According to Richard Dawkins (1976, p. 1), Darwin's theory provides an answer to the child's question: "Why are people?" This is just not correct. Darwin explains the "origin of species," not the "origin of life." He explains how evolution occurred but not how or why life occurred. If science cannot explain how or why life occurred, we cannot rule out the possibility that there is a divine plan.

Familiarity with the notion of natural selection leads some people to think of life as the product of a series of accidents. This may seem a reasonable proposition so long as our thinking is carried on within the framework of the natural laws that govern our particular universe. However, the way in which atoms and molecules are formed is *determined* by these laws. The same can be said for all possible varieties of such atoms and molecules, and ultimately for all possible varieties of biological systems. If the laws were different, the same outcomes could not occur, and in the absence of such laws, complex living systems could not evolve. Indeed, in the absence of such laws, it is impossible to conceive of the existence of anything.

An equally interesting axiom is that a different set of laws would determine a different universe. Indeed, the laws or rules could be varied infinitely, and it becomes clear that *our material universe and the life-forms in it are the product of a particular set of laws.* Moreover, it is equally clear that in many conceivable alternative universes, life would not be possible. This leads to the conclusion that life is not accidental. It is the product of a particular set of natural laws. Since this is so, we are entitled to wonder why these particular laws were chosen, and by whom.

References

Bandura, A. 1977. *Social learning theory.* Englewood Cliffs, N.J.: Prentice Hall.

Barratt, E. S. 1985. Impulsiveness subtraits: Arousal and information processing. In J. T. Spence and C. E. Izard (eds.), *Motivation, emotion and personality.* North Holland: Elsevier.

Bouchard, T. J., Lykken, D. T., McGue, M., Segal, N. L., and Tellegen, A. 1990. Sources of human psychological differences: The Minnesota study of twins reared apart. *Science*, 250, 223–228.

Broadhurst, P. L. 1959. The interaction of task difficulty and motivation. The Yerkes-Dodson law revived. *Acta Psychologica*, 16, 321–338.

Burt, C. 1949. The structure of mind: A review of the results of factor analysis. *British Journal of Educational Psychology*, 19, 100–114, 176–219.

Cattell, R. B. 1971. *Abilities: Their structure, growth and action.* Boston: Houghton Mifflin.

Cattell, R. B. 1987. *Intelligence: Its structure, growth and action.* New York: North Holland.

Cattell, R. B. 1995. The fallacy of five factors in the personality sphere. *The Psychologist*, 8, 207–208.

Cioffi, F. 1974. Was Freud a liar? *The Listener,* 7, February, 1974.

Claridge, G. S. 1967. *Personality and arousal.* Oxford: Pergamon.

Claridge, G. S. 1995. *Origins of mental illness.* Cambridge, MA: Malor Books ISHK.

Costa, P. T., and McCrae, R. R. 1985. *The NEO personality inventory manual.* Odessa, Fla.: Psychological Assessment Resources.

Costa, P. T., and McCrae, R. R. 1992. Four ways five factors are basic. *Personality and Individual Differences*, 13, 653–665.

Dawkins, R. 1976. *The selfish gene*. Oxford: Oxford University Press.

Digman, J. M., and Inouye, J. 1986. Further specification of the five robust factors of personality. *Journal of Personality and Social Psychology*, 50, 116–123.

Eaves, L. J., Eysenck, H. J., and Martin, N. G. 1989. *Genes, culture and personality: An empirical approach*. New York: Academic Press.

Eccles, J. C. 1969. *The inhibitory pathways of the central nervous system*. Liverpool: Liverpool University Press.

Eysenck, H. J. 1944. Types of personality–a factorial study of 700 neurotics. *Journal of Mental Science*, 90, 851–861.

Eysenck, H. J. 1953. *The structure of human personality*. London: Methuen.

Eysenck, H. J. 1957. *The dynamics of anxiety and hysteria*. London: Routledge and Kegan Paul.

Eysenck, H. J. 1967. *The biological basis of personality*. Springfield, Ill.: Thomas.

Eysenck, H. J. 1982. *A model for personality*. New York: Springer-Verlag.

Eysenck, H. J. 1992. Four ways five factors are *not* basic. *Personality and Individual Differences*, 13, 667–663.

Eysenck, H. J., and Eysenck, M. W. 1985. *Personality and individual differences: A natural science approach*. London: Plenum Press.

Eysenck, H. J., and Eysenck, S. B. G. 1975. *Manual of the Eysenck personality questionnaire*. London: Hodder and Stoughton.

Eysenck, H. J., and Eysenck, S. B. G. 1976. *Psychoticism as a dimension of personality*. London: Hodder and Stoughton.

Freud, S. 1953–1974. *The standard edition of the complete psychological works*. J. Strachey (ed.) London: Hogarth Press.

Goldberg, L. R. 1990. An alternative "description of personality": The Big-Five factor structure. *Journal of Personality and Social Psychology*, 59, 1216–1229.

Goldberg, L. R. 1993. The structure of phenotypic personality traits. *American Psychologist*, 48, 26–33.

Gray, J. A. 1964. Strength of the nervous system as a dimension of personality in man: A review of work from the laboratory of B. M. Teplov. In J. A. Gray (ed.), *Pavlov's Typology*. Oxford: Pergamon.

Gray, J. A. 1979. *Pavlov*. London: Fontana.

Gray, J. A. 1982. A critique of Eysenck's theory of personality. In H. J. Eysenck (ed.), A model for personality. New York: Springer-Verlag.

Haier, R. J., Robinson, D. L., Braden, W., and Williams, D. 1983. Electrical potentials of the cerebral cortex and psychometric intelligence. *Personality and Individual Differences*, 4, 591–599.

Haier, R. J., Robinson, D. L., Braden, W., and Williams, D. 1984. Evoked potential augmenting-reducing and personality differences. *Personality and Individual Differences*, 5, 293–301.

Hebb, D. O. 1949. *The organization of behaviour.* New York: Wiley.

Hebb, D. O. 1959. Intelligence, brain function and the theory of mind. *Brain,* 82, 260–275.

Hendrickson, D. E. 1982. The biological basis of intelligence. Part II: Measurement. In H. J. Eysenck (ed.), *A Model for Intelligence.* Berlin: Springer-Verlag.

Henneberg, M. 1987. Hominid cranial capacity change through time: A Darwinian process. *Human Evolution,* 2, 213–220.

Herrick, C. J. 1971. *The evolution of human nature.* Austin: University of Texas Press.

Hogan, R. 1986. *Hogan personality inventory manual.* Minneapolis, MN: National Computer Systems.

Hunt, E. B. 1980. Intelligence as an information-processing concept. *British Journal of Psychology,* 71, 449–474.

Jung, C. G. 1971. Psychological types. In H. Read, M. Fordham, G. Adler and W. McGuire (eds.), *Collected works,* Vol. 6. Translated by R. F. C. Hull. London: Routledge and Kegan Paul.

Koestler, A. 1967. *The ghost in the machine.* London: Hutchinson.

Kretschmer, E. 1948. *Korperbau und charakter.* Berlin: Springer.

Lewontin, R. C., Rose, S., and Kamin, L. J. 1984. *Not in our genes; biology, ideology, and human nature.* New York: Pantheon.

Loehlin, J. C. 1989. Partitioning environmental and genetic contributions to behavioral development. *American Psychologist,* 44, 1285.

Lynn, R. 1965. *Attention, arousal and the orientation reaction.* New York: Pergamon.

Lynn, R. 1990. The evolution of brain size and intelligence in man. *Human Evolution,* 5, 241–244.

Lynn, R., Wilson, G., and Gault, A. 1989. Simple musical tests as measures of Spearman's "g." *Personality and Individual Differences,* 10, 25–28.

Magoun, H. W. 1963. *The waking brain.* Springfield, Ill.: Thomas.

Mangan, G. L. 1980. *The biology of human conduct.* Oxford: Pergamon.

Maslow, A. H. 1968. *Toward a psychology of being.* Princeton, N.J.: Van Nostrand.

Mischel, W. 1976. *Introduction to personality.* New York: Holt, Rinehart and Winston.

Moruzzi, G., and Magoun, H. W. 1949. Brain stem reticular formation and activation of the EEG. *Electroencephalography and Clinical Neurophysiology,* 1, 455–473.

Nebylitsyn, V. D. 1972. *Fundamental properties of the human nervous system.* English translation edited by G. L. Mangan. New York: Plenum.

Norman, W. T. 1963. Toward an adequate taxonomy of personality attributes: Replicated factor structure in peer nomination personality ratings. *Journal of Abnormal and Social Psychology,* 66, 574–583.

Pavlov, I. P. 1930. A brief outline of the higher nervous activity. In C. A. Murchison (ed.), *Psychologies of 1930*. Worchester, MA.: Clark University Press.

Pavlov, I. P. 1955. *Selected works*. Translated by S Belsky. Moscow: Foreign Languages Publishing House.

Plomin, R., and Daniels, D. 1987. Why are children in the same family so different from one another? *Behavioural and Brain Sciences*, 10, 1–60.

Plomin, R., and Loehlin, J. C. 1989. Direct and indirect IQ heritability estimates: A puzzle. *Behavior Genetics*, 19, 331–342.

Pribram, K. H. 1968. Toward a neuropsychological theory of person. In K. H. Pribram (ed.), *The study of personality: An interdisciplinary approach*. New York: Holt, Rinehart and Winston.

Robinson, D. L. 1982. Properties of the diffuse thalamocortical system and human personality: A direct test of Pavlovian/Eysenckian Theory. *Personality and Individual Differences*, 3, 1–16.

Robinson, D. L. 1983. An analysis of human EEG responses in the alpha range of frequencies. *International Journal of Neuroscience*, 22, 81–98.

Robinson, D. L. 1985. How personality relates to intelligence test performance: Implications for a theory of intelligence, aging research and personality assessment. *Personality and Individual Differences*, 6, 203–216.

Robinson, D. L. 1986a. On the biological determination of personality structure. *Personality and Individual Differences*, 7, 435–438.

Robinson, D. L. 1986b. A commentary on Gray's critique of Eysenck's theory. *Personality and Individual Differences*, 7, 461–468.

Robinson, D. L. 1986c. The Wechsler Adult Intelligence Scale and personality assessment: Towards a biologically based theory of intelligence and cognition. *Personality and Individual Differences*, 7, 153–159.

Robinson, D. L. 1987. A neuropsychological model of personality and individual differences. In J. Strelau and H. J. Eysenck (eds.), *Personality dimensions and arousal*. London: Plenum Press.

Robinson, D. L. 1989. The neurophysiological basis of high IQ. *International Journal of Neuroscience*, 46, 209–234.

Robinson, D. L. 1991. On the neurology of intelligence and intelligence factors. In H. A. H. Rowe (ed.), *Intelligence: Reconceptualization and measurement*. London: Lawrence Erlbaum Associates.

Robinson, D. L. 1993. The EEG and intelligence: An appraisal of methods and theories. *Personality and Individual Differences*, 15, 695–716.

Robinson, D. L., and desRosiers, G. Differential recall of positively and negatively toned associates by sanguine and melancholic individuals. In preparation.

Robinson, D. L., Gabriel, N., and Katchan, O. 1994. Personality and second language learning. *Personality and Individual Differences*, 16, 143–157.

Robinson, D. L., Haier, R. J., Braden, W., and Krengel, M. 1984a. Evoked potential augmenting and reducing: The methodological and theoretical significance of new electrophysiological observations. *International Journal of Psychophysiology*, 2, 11–22.

Robinson, D. L., Haier, R. J., Braden, W., and Krengel, M. 1984b. Psychometric intelligence and visual evoked potentials: A replication. *Personality and Individual Differences*, 5, 487–489.

Rogers, C. R. 1980. *A way of being*. Boston: Houghton Mifflin.

Samuels, I. 1959. Reticular mechanisms and behaviour. *Psychological Bulletin*, 56, 1–25.

Scarr, S. 1987. Three cheers for behavior genetics: Winning the war and losing our identity. *Behavioral Genetics*, 17, 219–228.

Seligman, M. E. P. 1971. Phobias and preparedness. *Behaviour Therapy*, 2, 307–320.

Spearman, C. 1904. "General intelligence" objectively determined and measured. *American Journal of Psychology*, 15, 72–101.

Spearman, C. 1927. *The abilities of man*. London: Macmillan.

Sternberg, R. J. 1977. *Intelligence, information processing, and analogical reasoning: The componential analysis of human abilities*. Hillsdale, N.J.: Erlbaum.

Strelau, J. 1983. *Temperament personality activity*. London: Academic Press.

Teplov, B. M. 1964. Problems in the study of general types of higher nervous activity in man and animals. In J. A. Gray (ed.), *Pavlov's typology*. London: Pergamon.

Trapnell, P. D., and Wiggins, J. S. 1990. Extension of the Interpersonal Adjectives Scales to include the Big Five dimensions of personality. *Journal of Personality and Social Psychology*, 59, 781–790.

Vernon, P. A. 1993. *Biological approaches to the study of human intelligence*. New Jersey: Ablex Publishing Corporation.

Vogel, W., and Broverman, D. M. 1964. Relationship between EEG and test intelligence: A critical review. *Psychological Bulletin*, 62, 132–144.

von Bertalanffy, L. 1967. *Robots, Men and Minds: Psychology in the modern world*. Heinz Werner Memorial Lectures. New York: G. Braziller.

Webb, E. 1915 Character and intelligence. *British Journal of Psychology Monograph Series*, 1, no. 3

Yerkes, R. M., and Dodson, J. D. 1908. Relation of strength of stimulus to rapidity of habit formation. *Journal of Comparative Neurology and Psychology*, 18, 459–482.

Zuckerman, M. 1994. *Behavioral expressions and biosocial bases of sensation seeking:* New York: Cambridge University Press.

Index

About the Author

DAVID L. ROBINSON is Associate Professor in the Department of Community Medicine and Behavioural Sciences at Kuwait University. He has lectured and researched at the University of Sydney, the U.S. National Institute on Aging, and Brown University.

ISBN 0-275-95468-4

EAN

9 780275 954680

HARDCOVER BAR CODE